I0160382

Hey, Where's *My* Bailout?

5 Easy Steps to
Regain Control of Your Life in 60 Days

Todd Josko & Debbie Lundberg

Copyright 2009 by Debbie Lundberg

Debbie Lundberg, inc.

PO Box 13248

Tampa, FL 33681

ISBN: 978-0-578-00855-4

First Edition

All rights reserved. No part of this book may be reproduced or transmitted in any form or by any means, electronic or mechanical, including photocopying, recording, or by any information storage and retrieval system, without written permission from the authors, except for the inclusion of brief quotations in a presentation, review or article about the book or authors.

This material has been written and published solely for educational purposes. The authors shall have neither liability nor responsibility to any person or entity with respect to any loss, damage or injury caused or alleged to be caused directly or indirectly by the information contained in this book.

Cover and chapter illustrations by Cida Bormann. Cover design by Sue Nance.

Thank you Marcie Falco! Your work and abilities assisted us greatly in the editing and proofing of this book!

Hey, Where's *My* Bailout?

5 Easy Steps to

Regain Control of Your Life in 60 Days

Todd Josko & Debbie Lundberg

"Planning is bringing the future into the present so that you can do something about it now."

~ Alan Lakein

Contents

Introduction

Congratulations! You want to regain control of your life and bail yourself out of the situation you are in currently, whether personally or professionally, financially or introspectively. Welcome to a book that will give you the tools necessary to create your own bailout *for your own unique situation, time, and place in life.*

No matter what attracted you to this book, there are three general things in life that keep us from getting things done: 1) we don't know, 2) we don't know how and 3) we don't want to. Everything leads back to one of these three – everything. If something sounds or appears different, it is really just an excuse. So, resist the excuses and remember it is 1, 2 or 3. The approach to addressing each of these situations is different: 1) information, 2) coaching or training and 3) attitude check.

Within *Hey, Where's My Bailout?*, we will address all three situations by offering you 1) ideas and information, 2) coaching for sharing ways to appreciate what you have and change what you don't, and finally, 3) the right approach and steps for positioning your attitude for bailing out yourself. If at anytime you seem unsure of your bailout, go back to the three reasons and decide if you need more information, coaching, or an attitude check. You will quickly be back on track with your bailout...and eventually, your life!

Hey, Where's My Bailout? is both a narrative and a workbook, complete with ideas, activities, tips written in 1st or 3rd person (for a unique perspective from one or both of the writers), personal stories about people who used the steps for success, and a calendar through which you will interactively progress while reading and incorporating the ideas of the writers.

At the time of publication, the recent explosion of highly visible bailout rescue plans for corporate and financial institutions has caused more and more ordinary people to begin asking, "hey, where's *my* bailout?" While you are quite important and your impact is great, you are not a large financial institution or long lasting industry. The only bailout plan option you have had in the past was to consider bankruptcy. *No one is handing you a bailout*, whether you read this book in the midst of the government bailouts or later.

Hey, Where's My Bailout? is formatted to give you thoughts to consider and actionable items to design and relish in your own personal bailout plan. We, the authors, are not financial planners, hiring managers or psychiatrists. In addition, we are not condoning or condemning those who have been in, or are considering, bankruptcy as a solution to their personal financial situation. Instead, this book offers unique advice and solutions aimed toward regaining control of your life though reflection and tested plans, systems and procedures.

It is imperative to remember, though, with thoughts of big industry and government intervention top of mind, your bailout begins with YOU! Nobody's going to bail you out, for you, and you alone, are responsible for bailing out you.

By purchasing this book, you have taken the critical first step. We look forward to sharing our thoughts and ideas with you for the rest of your bailout journey...and eventual bailout success.

Your Bailout Begins with You

You may have found yourself watching one of the cable news channels at some point, seeing yet another company or industry seeking a bailout from the Federal Government. The parade of participants changes but the scenario remains constant - an entity or organization is looking for someone, in this case the U.S. taxpayers, to bail them out of an adverse situation.

In many instances, the bailout requests have begun long before the company in question appears before a Congressional Committee. The company may have first turned to customers, investors, employees or other stakeholders prior to seeking financial aid from the U.S. Government. The company executives may well have sought taxpayer aid as a last resort, only because all other options to date had failed. Or, situations may have deteriorated so badly within their organization that the Federal Government remained the only entity with enough resources to handle such a large-scale bailout.

While it may be hard for us to equate our own personal situations with those of large financial institutions or other federal bailout seekers, we can likely empathize with the lack of control these executives must feel when pleading their case before lawmakers. The end result - the future viability of their company - is out of their hands. The best that these executives can do is state their case and hope that someone else (the Government) will bail them out.

Certainly, strong arguments can be made about possible unwise or unethical business decisions made by some of the companies that now seek taxpayer aid. While it is not our intent to opine on whether particular bailouts are truly deserved, we want to focus instead on the dynamics surrounding the bailout request.

This lack of control of one's fate is our key focus. Regardless of our agreement or disagreement with the merits of a particular bailout, we can agree that this lack of control is not an enviable situation for anyone to experience.

Often in our lives, it seems that our fate lies in someone else's hands. If we have a career that appears secure on the surface, we must still acknowledge that changes in technology, political landscape or company finances could suddenly shatter that perceived security at any moment's notice. If our importance to a given organization is based on someone else's priorities, a change in those priorities can render our importance diminished…or even insignificant.

If we surrender our fate to the decisions of others, then poor decisions that get made, even without our knowledge or buy-in, can have devastating consequences to our personal well being. As executives who have gone before Congress experienced, allowing someone else to choose winners and losers is not a plan....it's a risky recipe for disaster.

Typically when we think of bailouts we think of finances. It is easy to believe that money can solve all problems and that all bailouts are financial in nature, but this is not solely the case. Consider the plight of the automakers. While there were certainly issues of accountability and debate as to whether these companies individually or collectively deserved taxpayer funds, Congress seemed most hesitant to give them a financial bailout because many Members were concerned with the viability of profitable business models going forward. Decision makers were worried that American automakers too frequently produce cars that consumers simply do not want, and will not buy.

Common sense and Business 101 tell us that private companies must turn a profit in order to succeed. Members of Congress feared that if consumers ultimately don't want the cars produced by U.S. automakers, then the U.S. automakers would not sell enough cars to maintain long term profits and sustainability. So, however much money was loaned to them, Members voiced concern that the automakers would burn through the money in short order and come back looking for more in the not-so-distant future. When this book went to print, the concerns about U.S. automakers' additional requests were becoming a reality. Many lawmakers were arguing the need for comprehensive change to business plans from American automakers…and not just a hand-out.

Any long-term bailout solution must address comprehensive change. Plans, procedures and systems must be designed and implemented which offer a roadmap to success. In the case of the automakers, the companies that sought one or more bailouts were being required to show that they had a plan in place to produce and market cars that would be attractive to consumers and increase sales. The bailout loan from the taxpayers, regardless of the amount of funding, served only as a short-term bridge designed to keep solvency until plans, procedures and systems were in place and profitability was restored. Without those fundamentals, cash would eventually run out once again and the company, or companies, would be right back where they started.

Have you ever read about someone who wins millions in the lottery only to find themselves broke again in a few years? These unfortunate stories happen all the time. Another sad but somewhat common story, is the one of the professional actor or athlete who makes tens of millions of dollars over a career, only to find themselves penniless when their playing and/or acting days are over. In any case, the initial windfall of cash flow was short-lived, no matter how large the amount, because the person had no systems in place designed to orchestrate true long-term success – financially or emotionally, personally or professionally.

For most people in need of a bailout, money may be a short-term need - often a critical need - but it's almost never the long-term answer. If you were to receive a one-time lump sum cash bailout, how long would it last? If you are like most people, money never lasts as long as you think it will or need it to. At some point, maybe in a year or maybe in a month, your savings would run out (unless you've been fortunate enough to accumulate generational wealth in your lifetime – and if so, it is a surprise that this book is in your hands!) For the rest of us, the key to a successful bailout is creating those plans, procedures and systems that create a blueprint for a different and more successful way of conducting our lives, each and every day.

This blueprint does not simply apply to a financial bailout, though that is typically the type of bailout plan we often hear about in these uncertain times. You may need to create a bailout plan to rescue your marriage or to attain a healthy weight. Whatever the need, your approach to problems (up to this point) has not been working, or you have had success in one, or some areas, and not in others. Throwing money at the situation, or simply trying harder, has not worked or is not applicable.

For true change to take place, you will take the time to look hard at how you arrived at this point in your life, recognize that you need to create your own bailout, and then put plans, procedures, and systems in place that will give you the tools to live the life you always imagined.

Learn from the Crisis Managers

Life is full of the unexpected. No one knows for sure what lies ahead because life is full of surprises – both good and bad.

Crisis managers and public relations professionals often assist companies and organizations to better prepare for the unexpected by helping them craft a crisis response plan. For example, if a company suddenly faced claims that a product was unsafe, what would be the steps taken to reassure the minds of the public, media, customers or other stakeholders? Who would be the person or persons in the organization responsible for communicating to each of these audiences, and how would they do it rapidly and effectively?

A well-prepared crisis response plan puts plans, procedures and systems in place *before* the unexpected occurs. Listing specific action item steps and assigning responsibilities, in writing, allows organizations to better anticipate potential unexpected scenarios and better control unexpected situations that otherwise might control them.

Many individuals have a crisis plan in, although they may not recognize it as such. Insurance is a type of crisis plan – you prepare for the unexpected by paying insurance premiums and should the unexpected occur, the insurance company pays benefits, repairs or cash to you or your beneficiary. A retirement account, or even a savings account, can be a crisis plan as well. Many people suffering in today's economy have used either, or both accounts, as their crisis plan to compensate for lack of employment or income. Whether they realized it at the time or not, the money they put away each month was their preparation for the unexpected economic crisis that exists today.

In talking with organizations or individuals, the common denominator for a crisis plan is preparation. The more we prepare, the greater our chance of successfully managing the crisis. With preparation, while we cannot *guarantee* success, we can significantly increase our *probability* of success.

One Man's Crisis is Another Man's Bailout

The Roman philosopher Seneca stated, "luck is what happens when preparation meets opportunity." We interpret that to mean, to a very large extent, you create your own luck. You create such luck through preparation and opportunity. The intersection between the two is *luck* or the good fortune outcome that results from the combination of the two.

Both of the factors – preparation and opportunity can be managed. You can consciously, or sometimes even unconsciously, increase the amount of preparation you do. You can also increase the amount of opportunity in which you place yourself. Adding both together, you can dramatically increase the probability of good fortune arising.

Luck still exists when the good fortune outcome defies the odds of preparation and opportunity. Every week someone wins the lottery in spite of infinitesimal odds. And sometimes the best laid plans go awry. But by and large, the degree to which you prepare and place yourself in opportunity's way are the surest ways to achieve "luck."

If you were a student in class you would have the opportunity to demonstrate your mastery of a topic by taking an exam. You would prepare for this opportunity by studying and, assuming you did a good job preparing, you would receive a good grade on the exam. But you would not consider your good grade "luck." In fact, calling your result luck would be a bit of an insult because it minimizes the preparation you undertook to achieve your good fortune – the good grade.

Earning a good grade on a surprise or "pop" quiz may seem more like luck to outsiders because the opportunity to demonstrate knowledge was unexpected. Your classmates may say you were lucky, but you know that the same determinate of success was your degree of preparation. Whether you knew the opportunity was coming or not was irrelevant.

Taking the opportunity to demonstrate your preparedness is seizing the moment and taking action. In effect, each time you have had a pop quiz and succeeded, you had a bailout plan in place that led to your success. Paying attention in class and learning the material through lectures and projects was your preparation. The quiz was your opportunity.

So, as Seneca and others have hypothesized, there is not a lucky break or a luck factor that you can look for, hope for or especially rely on in your life. Like the exams and pop quizzes, *your preparation is your plan to successfully seize upon opportunity.*

"Being deeply learned and skilled, being well trained and using well spoken words; this is good luck."

~ Buddha

Bailout and Beyond Tip #1
Don't Call Me Lucky...

While it is tempting to think of others as lucky and you, personally, as unlucky, it really just is not the case. Unless someone was walking down the street and found $50, it is typically insulting to call someone lucky...especially when you do not know the background and efforts that got someone where she or he is today.

When I was in high school, subsequently taking courses at the local campus of the University of Michigan preparing to go "away" to school in Ann Arbor, MI, one of my friends and I made plans for where we were going to live in Ann Arbor, and we imagined how much fun it was going to be living together. We had everything all figured out...or so I thought. One day, my friend came to me and said she was not going "away". She wanted to stay close to home (read as "close to her boyfriend" at the time), and said that I was going to have to either stay home too, or go "away" by myself. At the time, the University of Michigan had about 43,000 students, so I knew I would not be "by myself", and since I had prepared for it, and being on campus would be a wonderful opportunity, I went.

My grandfather died unexpectedly the summer before I was planning to move to Ann Arbor, and since the day of his funeral was the same day I scheduled to meet my prospective new roommate, I left after the funeral to drive, heavy-hearted, in hopes of meeting a new, normal, somewhat-friendly person with whom I would spend day and night sharing a small space. I drove on I-69 to US-23 to

14 crying intermittently over the loss of my grandfather and the disappointment in my friend's decision to bail on me. When I met my future roommate, she couldn't have been nicer, kinder or more willing to show me around campus, and even share a fourth-floor room.

Years later, after growing my education, exposure and friendships in Ann Arbor, I returned to where I grew up and began working. My friend whom had not gone away to school with me was still in school, not with her boyfriend of years past, still living with her mom, and wondering what she wanted to do with her future. She came over to my 650 sq. ft. apartment where I had decorated it with new furniture from my earnings as an intern and my first new "real job".

I was proud of how my work had paid off. She was sitting on my loveseat and she casually looked around for a bit and proclaimed, "you're so lucky!" Almost instantly, I smiled and insisted "I'm a lot of things, but please, if you still want to be friends, do not ever call me lucky again." I shared with her "I did not feel lucky when you backed out on me. I did not feel lucky to leave my grandfather's wake to drive in hopes a stranger would meet me like she said she would, and be a good roommate. I was not feeling lucky when I had surgery at the University without family because something was found that had to be addressed immediately. I did not feel lucky wandering around thinking how much fun we'd have in Ann Arbor. I wasn't lucky to be driving in snow to get to my parents' home to do my laundry. And, definitely getting a job over so many other qualified people wasn't lucky!"

Luck is when you don't know and either don't deserve or care about the outcome. I was prepared…even for the worst with my adventurous, positive attitude, drive and focus. When the opportunity came to capitalize and embrace the timing and the education/experience, I did not rely on luck…I relied on me…me to say yes, me to take the first step, me to take the next step and every step there after to get from point A to point B. I love that I still have a good relationship with my friend from high school when I see her…and I'd confidently lay money on the table to bet anyone that she would never call me lucky again!

The same is true for you…respect where people are, ask if they like how they got there, and appreciate their efforts. No matter how lucky someone may appear, there was preparation and opportunity mixed in at different percentages, but it is highly unlikely that it was *just luck*!

Your Bailout Awaits You!

When preparation is unknown or opportunity is unexpected, outsiders like to view the good fortune result as a fluke or a surprise. But the wise person knows that opportunity and preparation can be controlled and leveraged. The more you prepare, and the more often you place yourself in situations to reap the benefits of good fortune, the more success you will have.

What others see as luck, you can now see as a bailout plan. *This intersection of preparation and opportunity is the key to your bailout plan.*

The opportunities that come to you in life may be expected or unexpected, but you will not receive good fortune outcomes unless you are prepared. Without preparation, your bailout will fail. This book will guide you through how to prepare your bailout plan.

Similarly, you can prepare all you want, but unless you have opportunity, your preparation will be in vein. This book will also show you how to create your own opportunities.

In five easy steps, we will teach you to:

- *Assess* how prior preparation, or lack thereof, led you to your current point in life,

- *Prioritize* what types of preparation you will need to best pursue the opportunities you seek,

- **L*everage*** your preparation to create or expand new opportunities,

- ***Communicate*** and create more opportunity by allowing others to know your plan and assist you, and to

- ***Act*** because you, and you alone, are responsible for creating your own preparation and opportunity.

So what are you waiting for? Your bailout plan awaits!

How This Book Works

Hey, Where's My Bailout? is very different from most other self-help, guidance or instructional books. Sure, sure, we sound like proud parents bragging that a child is gifted or special compared to everyone else, but here is how our approach is unique.

Hey, Where's My Bailout? is a truly interactive experience that provides an idea, followed by an activity, combining a real-life story and offering sound direction based on you; your own, personal answers and interests. We're sincere in stating *you*, because *you* will be creating your plan based on what we provide.

The chapters will begin with an announcement of each step, followed by a quotation to inspire thought and focus on the topic at hand. At the start of each chapter, that step will be identified and defined for the purposes of this book. We will share the reasoning behind each step, and offer a preview of the activities.

From there, a discussion of the step and its importance to your bailout plan will be outlined. Each chapter will include a story about someone who successfully completed (or is completing at the time of this publication) each step, some commentary, an idea or two to better illustrate the step, and key activities and actions for you to complete. Can you get a lot out of the book by just reading and not completing the activities? Sure, you'll gain knowledge, but knowledge alone is just a bit of fact or opinion. That old expression *knowledge is power* is far from the truth - the reality is that *the application of knowledge is powerful*. So with that, we strongly recommend you *apply* your knowledge, complete the activities, and unleash your powerful bailout plan.

For best results, you are well served to write directly in your book. Be honest…meaning be truthful with the person who matters most…you. Please do not attempt to sugarcoat responses or craft answers that only seem good. This book is written for you to be you…and any dishonesty or deception will ultimately undermine your efforts to create your own successful bailout plan. Your competencies and idiosyncrasies alike help make you unique and different. Embrace your self-perceived assets and shortcomings and take comfort in knowing that by completing these exercises you are finding the answers within you to regain control of your life.

Finally, when you get through the first four steps, and nearly done with the fifth and final step, you will find a 60 day calendar that you will complete. You will produce a workable calendar by using ideas, responses, processes and plans from the previous chapters, filling in the blanks, and following through on your commitment *to you…to your bailout plan. Hey, Where's My Bailout?* is designed to be an easy, interesting and entertaining book. If you are willing to look within yourself and offer honest insight and thoughtful responses, we will show you how to use five easy steps to create your own personal bailout plan in only 60 days!

Let's get started…

Step 1: ASSESS

"The object of reflection is invariably the discovery of something satisfying to the mind which was not there at the beginning of the search."

~ Ernest Dimnet

Step 1: Assess

Assess how prior preparations, or lack thereof, led you to your current point in life.

Reason: *Assess* is the first step is for perspective and positioning. It is like peeling an apple - you have to start at the beginning. While we considered words like reflect and evaluate, we did not select those. It is imperative in any situation, prior to committing, sharing, or doing something else that one assess the situation, the people, the consequences and the rewards prior to actually doing anything (other than inquiring). *Assess* comes before other steps in this book because it is your foundation directionally, and will be the base for guiding you to your answers, and eventually your plan.

Activities: Life Area Review, Cycle of Self, Strengths and Opportunities Traits Assessment.

Albert Einstein is quoted as having said that if he had one hour to save the world he would spend fifty-five minutes defining the problem and only five minutes finding the solution. Whether we are trying to solve complex public policy issues or creating a bailout plan for our own personal situation, Einstein's observation remains relevant.

It is foolish and counter-productive to dive right into the solving of any problem unless you first thoroughly examine the current situation and factors that contributed to the present being. Only then, once the current situation is known and understood more clearly, can we begin to create our plans, procedures and systems designed to bring about change in our lives.

If we skip this first critical step of assessing our current situation, we run the risk of creating a bailout plan that fails to meet our needs or fails to adequately address the changes we seek.

A road map is a great tool for driving direction, but it can only be of proper benefit if we know exactly where we are *beginning* our trip. It is not enough to just know where we are going. We must know from where we are starting in order to find the best path to our destination.

The same principle holds true for creating your bailout plan. You cannot properly identify your possible solutions, and then chose your best possible solution, until you correctly assess your current situation.

It has been said that *progress has little to do with speed but much to do with direction.* Let's begin to create your bailout plan by first assessing where you are, and what direction you want to go.

Bailout and Beyond Tip #2
BE/DO/HAVE...It's Up to You!

Once each of us meets our basic physical needs of food, shelter, and comfort, we typically passively or actively look to "find" happiness.

We are often unknowingly participating in the HAVE/DO/BE approach to happiness. This is the process of acting on the notion or belief of once I HAVE the money/status/things I need, I will DO great/fun/cool/meaningful things and therefore, BE happy.

If this is your approach, for whatever conscious or subconscious reason, I challenge you to reverse the approach by adopting the BE/DO/HAVE approach to life. (Yes, life, which is more than "happiness".)

With the BE/DO/HAVE methodology of living a personally guided and intentional life, you would decide to BE whatever feelings you want, DO the things within your means and therefore, HAVE what you want and need. As a realistic person, I do not suggest you claim pure happiness in the face of adversity or only anticipate silver linings all day long. Rather, I purport that seeking, identifying and embracing "what works for you" and the happiness in each experience you have, will allow you to raise your base of vision and perspective and enable you to appreciate what is presented and keep gratefulness in close proximity to happiness.

In the DO category of this approach, I have heard so many people profess it would be easier to do more with more money and *how couldn't one be happy when they have money,* but rest assured, that simply is not the case.   Money truly does not buy happiness. Still, when I hear something like "there is no sense in going to a game because I can only afford the nose bleed seats", it is the person who marvels at the joy of the game and being there…regardless of the location, who truly has the DO approach…and does it. Likewise, if you figure when you have a new job or career, you will do the things you "should" and be the person others expect, you are working against your own success…

With the HAVE aspect, it is about enjoying and focusing on what you have instead of focusing on what you do not have.   Sure I do not have the money for a personal chef, but I do have a husband who is a terrific and generous grill master, so I look at what I have and it follows that even more comes to me.   Similarly, if you say I will HAVE happiness, *that* is impossible. Happiness is a BE state because there is an active level of engagement and participation in it. Having the perspective and attention to detail to enjoy, embrace and encourage, is in the HAVE.

Should you find yourself thinking, "if only I were to HAVE the right parents, car, SUV, house, shoes, job, career, manager, leader, etc., then I would be able to DO so much more and BE happy," you have a choice: act the same as you have in the past, and know that you will continually want to HAVE something more to allow you to DO things in your demands and expectations to BE happy, or act differently for and with yourself and turn around the flow to decide to BE happy with what you are and to DO things for yourself and then, not surprisingly, you will HAVE all you need and likely all you want, too. The choice is yours to make. Your bailout plan depends on such choices, DO, BE, and then HAVE your own bailout plan.

Self Assessment Starts Here

Without reflection and assessment, we are not aware of where we have been or where we are going. People who do not assess where they are and what is happening become victims of complaint, blame or even distain for their situation, people or both.

When reflecting on aspects of life such as situations, relationships, results, mishaps or successes, there exists a bias…a personal view of how things should have been or could have been. We are asking you to be aware of your bias during these assessments and use them for what can be done in the future, what is realistic and what you want to be.

While you will take some time to look back, the time for assessing is part reflection and part projecting so that you learn from the past, avoid similar mistakes in the future, repeat solid performances in the future and set yourself up for success in your bailout plan.

Imagine if you did not review where you are now…how would you determine where your starting point is? If you did not anticipate where you are going, what would you do first to get on the right path? The self-assessment exercises get your ideas aligned with your thoughts, so that your behaviors, and therefore, *your results*, will follow.

When you look to bail yourself out financially, emotionally, physically or mentally, your plan must begin with a determination of where you are at the present and where your successful plan will take you. It is often said you must start with the end in mind, but we believe *if you do not start with the now in mind, your end will not mind you*!

Activity: Life Area Review I

Thinking of your true feelings, thoughts and behaviors, please consider each of the following 16 areas of your life and then record a numeric assessment of your current state next to each field. Determine each numerical reflection as a 1, 2, 3, 4 or 5, where 1 reflects the lowest level of satisfaction and 5 indicates the greatest level of satisfaction by area. There are no wrong answers (this is an assessment, not a test), and for the best results, record your first instinct, and resist changing responses.

The areas are defined as:

Self-Confidence – The degree to which you feel good about you, your approach, your choices, and your results.

Career – The field, industry or company that you are a part of each day. You may work within your home, work for yourself, work for a company, or be starting a new career.

Self-Image/Style – The way you convey yourself. How you present, as a total package from the inside-out.

Communication – How you speak, write, share, and get messages across to one or many.

Friends – The people with whom you choose to surround yourself, their impact on you, and vice versa.

Health – How your overall state of health and wellness is based on medical reports and how you feel.

Organization – Your ability to know where things are, how to get things done, and keep on task.

Passion – Knowing what you enjoy, what you love, and having an interest and drive related to it that enhances your happiness and purpose.

Financial – Your money and your preparedness for the future financially.

Family – The people related to you, and how your relationships with them are impacting your life.

Love Life – Your intimate relationships with others and with yourself as a person.

Body – Your endurance and your perception of your body's appearance and capabilities.

Focus/Direction – Selecting things to do that are beneficial and appropriate for you. Being on the path you are on, including set goals and steps to move to and through the next part of your plan.

Emotions – Your ability to be reasonable. Your approach to taking things in stride and adjusting well to change.

Spirit – Your religious and personal preferences and views. How you are spending time on your spirituality and energy.

Habits – The things you do on a daily, weekly or monthly basis, which are part of your routine. These may be good or bad habits for you.

The 17th square, the one in the middle, is for your overall satisfaction – your satisfaction with your life in general. This is the culmination of the 16 areas, and scores, that precede it.

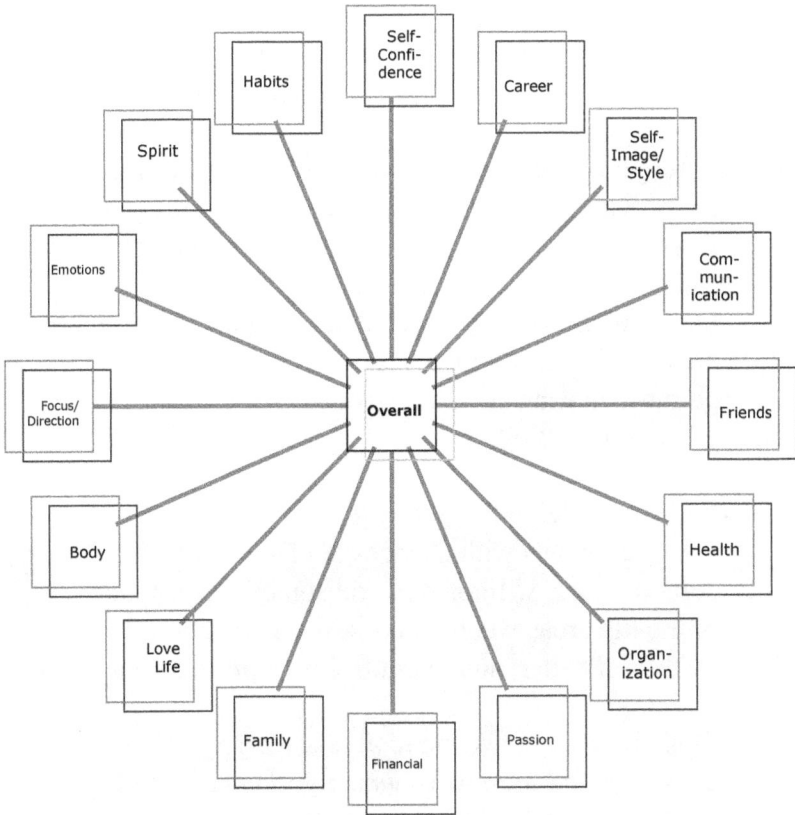

Activity: Life Area Review II

Now, copy your assessment scores from Part I to Part II under the "Score" columns.

Think of where you would like to be on that same range of 1 – 5, and record those numbers where the "Desire" column is. Where you Desire to be should reflect what is attainable and realistic for you. There are still no wrong answers here, since this is for you, and for you to use to motivate you to, and through, the next steps in your bailout plan.

After you have transferred you current scores from the previous page, and determined what score you Desire, note something you feel you are good at in each life area under the "Well" column. You do things Well even if you rated yourself a "1". You are already successful and good at many things, so go through each area, and give yourself credit for what you do Well.

Finally, while you do many great things, each life area presents us with chances to change. In the column labeled "Improve" add something for each of the life areas where you know you could make stride, get better, and overall, show improvement.

This process allows you to assess where you are currently, and introduces where you would like to go. You are recording it in an effort to make a commitment (minimally to you at this point), and you will share some things that will come from this later after some of the other steps.

An example is following the form below so that you can use the completed sheet as a guide.

Area	Score	Desire	Well	Improve
Self-Confidence	____	____	_____	_____
Career	____	____	_____	_____
Self-Image/Style	____	____	_____	_____
Communication	____	____	_____	_____
Friends	____	____	_____	_____
Health	____	____	_____	_____
Organization	____	____	_____	_____
Passion	____	____	_____	_____
Financial	____	____	_____	_____
Family	____	____	_____	_____
Love Life	____	____	_____	_____
Body	____	____	_____	_____
Focus/Direction	____	____	_____	_____
Emotions	____	____	_____	_____
Spirit	____	____	_____	_____
Habits	____	____	_____	_____
Overall	____	____	_____	_____

Life Area Review Part I Example

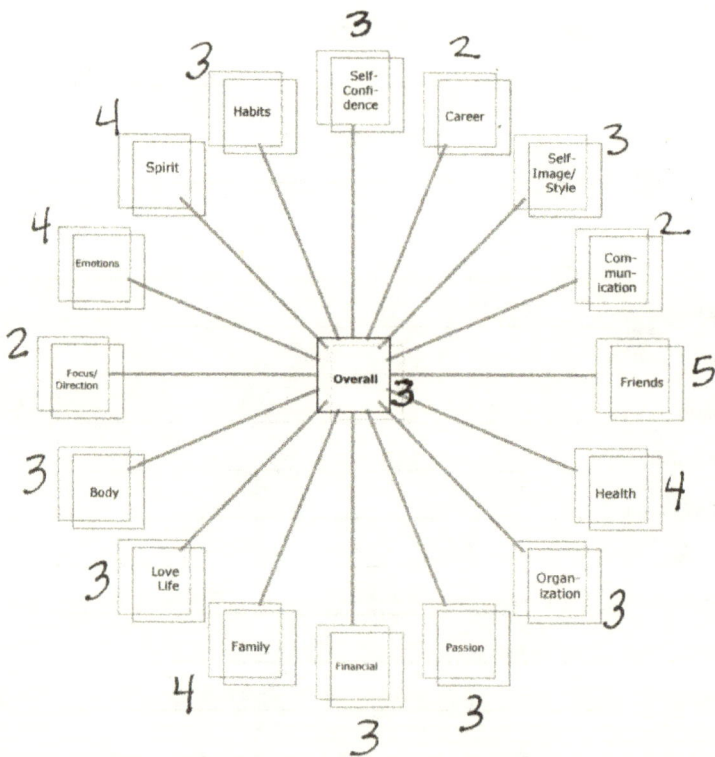

Life Area Review Part II Example

Area	Score	Desire	Well	Improve
Self-Confidence	3	5	asserting	Tact
Career	2	5	Job	Career
Self-Image/Style	3	5	Presenting	Doubt
Communication	2	4	Written	Verbal
Friends	5	5	Participating	staying intouch
Health	4	5	Weight	Heart health
Organization	3	5	home	office
Passion	3	5	Imagine	act on it
Financial	3	4	Savings	diversifying
Family	4	5	Interaction	sharing love
Love Life	3	5	dating	serious relationship
Body	3	5	Workouts	Intensity
Focus/Direction	2	4	stability	Where to go next
Emotions	4	5	Calm	Not speaking up
Spirit	4	4	Beliefs	Time meditating
Habits	3	4	Workouts	Business Networking
Overall	3	5	Surviving	Thriving

Activity: Cycle of Self

There are a variety of ways we self promote, self-sabotage or just maintain our status quo when we live our lives.   In the next assessment, you will be looking at your Cycle of Self.

Without reading ahead, and using just the definitions below, assess how much of your time per week is spent in each aspect of Self (remember, this is not where you would like to be or think you should be, rather, *where you are right now*.)   Bias plays a part in your Cycle of Self assessment, so think as objectively as possible on this, and all activities.

Selfless – Caring for others without regard for self.

Self-conscious – Moving through life with a sense of not belonging or what is wrong (discomfort) and/or seeking approval/position.

Self-exam – Looking at life and self for what is working and what can be improved (assessing).

Selfishness - Taking care of self without anticipation/expectation of others taking care of you.

Self-aware - Being in a state of openness and familiarity with the idea that action is next.

Self-respect - Acting and owning actions and outcomes for what makes you happy.

Self-confident - Owning actions/outcomes for your happiness without defense or need for awareness or approval from others while respecting them.

Self-serving - Taking care of self and interests with little regard for others or impact on others.

Self-absorbed – Solely taking care of self and interests without regard for others or impact on others, no matter the consequence.

Self-worship – Belief that self is greater than others with little or no reflection or consideration.

Here is a form for you, and there is an example on the next page to use as a guide.

Cycle of Self Review

Area	%	Desire	Keep	Change
Selfless				
Self-Conscious				
Self-Exam				
Selfishness				
Self-Aware				
Self-Respect				
Self-Confident				
Self-Serving				
Self-Absorbed				
Self-Worship				

Consider that when you get yourself in the desired state for you, your self-sufficiency will rise and your bailout plan will begin to be heading in the direction you want.

Cycle of Self Review Example

Area	%	Desire	Keep	Change
Selfless	29	15	Caring for others	Say no
Self-Conscious	18	10	Being interested	Being (un)comfortable
Self-Exam	14	14	Looking to grow	take action
Selfishness	5	20	Things for me	once a week
Self-Aware	7	15	figuring things out	Move fast
Self-Respect	8	10	Action	Define happy
Self-Confident	8	13	assert ideas	Share w/ others
Self-Serving	4	1	New things	Pay attention
Self-Absorbed	5	1	Free Spirit	Think of others
Self-Worship	2	1	Confidence	Reality check

Activity: Your Top Three

Just like you have life areas that are going well, and areas in the Cycle of Self in which you are achieving desired levels, you have wonderful strengths, and you also have opportunities to improve in other areas. Sometimes such things are innate, and other times they are learned, but nonetheless, there are traits we consistently do well, and in other areas we have a lot of room for growth. This is the time to determine which of your traits are strengths and which traits are opportunities for more growth.

First, record the trait, such as kindness, determination, compassion, drive, or any other attributes, that you see as your top 3 strengths:

1. _____

2. _____

3. _____

Second, record the traits, such as punctuality, blurting, consideration, or any other attributes that you see as your top 3 opportunities for improvement:

1. _____

2. _____

3. _____

Lastly, ask four to ten people who you admire, respect or trust to provide input for you on what each of them see as your top three strength traits and top three opportunity traits. Resist sharing with those people what you perceive as your strength traits and opportunity traits, as to not influence their input.

When asking for input, let each family member, friend, colleague, coach or mentor know what you admire about them, and share that you are in the process of improving yourself. (These same people, as well as others, are good resources, to revisit in *Step 3: Leverage.)*

Record the first part of the feedback below:

Strength Traits

(Yours)	(Yours)	(Yours)
_____	_____	_____
(Others)	(Others)	(Others)

1. _____ _____ _____
2. _____ _____ _____
3. _____ _____ _____
4. _____ _____ _____
5. _____ _____ _____
6. _____ _____ _____
7. _____ _____ _____
8. _____ _____ _____
9. _____ _____ _____
10. _____ _____ _____

Now record your opportunity traits feedback below.

Opportunity Traits

(Yours)	(Yours)	(Yours)
_____	_____	_____
(Others)	(Others)	(Others)

1. _____ _____ _____
2. _____ _____ _____
3. _____ _____ _____
4. _____ _____ _____
5. _____ _____ _____
6. _____ _____ _____
7. _____ _____ _____
8. _____ _____ _____
9. _____ _____ _____
10. _____ _____ _____

You are done with this activity for now. Think about what you have learned, what was surprising to discover and what was not. Space is provided here to record your responses to the input so that you reflect on what you have already gained:

Surprised me: _____

Something I anticipated: _____

This activity will be expanded upon in the next step
– *Prioritize*.

Casey Wohl – The Getaway Girl™

Girls Getaway Guide to Orlando
Leave Your Baggage At Home

Casey Wohl

What are the top five things you want to do, see or experience in your life before you die?

Casey Wohl found herself considering this question while attending a life-coaching seminar in 2006. Recent personal and professional challenges led Casey to re-assess her true priorities, and create a new life path which could combine her passions for travel and writing with her desire to own her own business. And that's just what she did.

"I was planning a girl's getaway trip with friends and began researching what to do in each city," says Casey. "Much to my surprise, there were no city-specific travel guides just for women, although these guides exist for other demographics."

Casey not only discovered a niche opportunity, she found a way to implement her newly assessed priorities. Plus, it was going to be a lot of fun.

Casey published her first book, the *Girls Getaway Guide to Orlando: Leave Your Baggage at Home®*, in September 2007, focusing on the area's best "girl-friendly" places to see, stay, shop, dine and spa. Since then, The Getaway Girl™ has penned an additional book for Key West with several more cities on the way. She has appeared on nationally syndicated television shows and in national publications providing advice for travelers everywhere. She is also a contributing writer for several online publications such as GoGirlfriend.com, Girlfriendology.com and Fabulously40.com, and has expanded her tagline, "Leave Your Baggage at Home®" to designer shirts, hats and other collateral materials.

Today, The Getaway Girl's™ website www.GirlsGetawayGuide.net is considered one of the top travel sites for women, and Casey Wohl is a nationally recognized expert on girlfriend getaways. She is also a big believer in taking time to assess, or re-assess, what is really important in life.

"Had I not consciously sat down and asked myself how to combine my goals of travel, writing and self-employment, I would not be where I am today," says Casey, "Instead, I would have likely accepted another salaried position in my previous profession of public relations." (Casey was formally a communications executive with the Florida citrus industry.) "I would have been content, but not truly happy. True happiness came by doing what I love to do."

Look for Casey's next Girls Getaway Guide to Nashville: Leave Your Baggage at Home® on bookshelves soon. She'll continue to seek new destinations, and continually reach new heights.

Step 2: **PRIORITIZE**

"Organizing is what you do before you do something, so that when you do it, it is not all mixed up."

~ A. A. Milne

Step 2: Prioritize

Prioritize what types of preparation you'll need to best pursue the opportunities you seek.

Reason: *Prioritize* is the second step for identifying where time should be spent, and getting the plan heading in a direction that has purpose to you, the reader and bailout creator. Other words or steps we considered were organize and clarify, but *Prioritize* does both in putting order or flow in the system, and bringing clarity to where things are in relation to goals and plans for the future. *Prioritize* comes after *Assess* because it takes what is discovered, uncovered or recognized and gives it order and weight so that an inappropriate amount of time is not spent on something that is not as valuable or as important to the plan.

Activities: Availability, Selection and Values, Assessing Interests, Planned Accomplishments.

Nearly every business advice book on the market addresses fundamental differences between Leadership and Management. We like to simplify the difference down to an analogy about trains: leadership is deciding where Point A and Point B are, and management gets the train from Point A to Point B.

In other words, leadership is about setting direction or goals while management is more concerned with accomplishing those directions or goals. For your bailout plan, think of the previous chapter of *Assess* as an exercise in leadership. You assessed what values and roles were truly important to you, and what direction your bailout plan will pursue.

Now it's time to zero in on the management function of *prioritizing* your activities. You have an idea of where you are heading, you now want to figure out the best way of getting there. That is the concept of prioritizing – determining the most appropriate steps and activities in order to best accomplish your assessed goals and values.

Much of the self-help literature written to date focuses on best practices for prioritization. Whether the discussion revolves around time management, the differentiation between important matters and immediate matters, suggestions on how to delegate in order to accomplish more daily activities or other similar topics, solutions always seem to revolve around sound planning and personal accountability.

And these solutions usually hold true, except for somewhere between best intentions and best results, daily life gets in the way and planning and accountability too often fall victim. Rather than rehash and repackage a lot of well-documented advice on productivity theory, we illustrate how prioritization can succeed in the real world and offer activities designed to enable you to incorporate these prioritization strategies into your bailout plan.

Ernest Hemmingway once said, "Never mistake motion for action." If action brings you closer to your assessed destination, then motion is the distraction that keeps you from getting there. Prioritize action. Eliminate motion.

A Great Monday Begins Sunday Night

We both love our weekends. No matter how much work either one of us has, no matter how far behind we may be on personal projects, we still like to let everything go on Saturdays (especially Todd). Both of us find that we are often extremely tempted to work on Saturdays, even Sundays, to get "caught up" but we rarely do.

Now we are not referring to the work presentation that is due first thing Monday morning which requires weekend preparation. Nor are we referring to the completion of yard work, or cleaning out the garage or other tasks best suited for the weekend. We are talking about routine work that never seems to get finished during working hours, Monday through Friday. Things that there "never seems to be enough hours in the day to finish." Things that can always be pushed back to Saturday.

We all know people who are workaholics. They spend a good part of their weekend in the office, or at home, working on myriad projects. While such dedication seems noble and desirable, the reality of weekend work is that an entire day (or days) gets dedicated but very little work gets accomplished. There is lots of motion, but very little action.

When our friends spend Saturday at the office, we love to ask them what they actually did all day. We want specifics. What time did you arrive at the office? Were you on the Internet at all? Did you go out for lunch, etc? Nearly every time we quiz our friends in such a manner, we usually discover that the person really only accomplished about an hour or so of actual work stretched over a full day. Most of their time is usually spent on busywork or time-wasting activities like paying bills online, surfing the net, organizing their desk or talking to other friends on the phone. At the end of the day, he or she could have accomplished the same amount of work by staying an extra hour on a Tuesday night rather than dedicating an entire Saturday.

As mentioned earlier, we do not profess to be psychiatrists, but we both know there is some pattern of self-punishment exhibited in this type of behavior. It seems that often people work on the weekends more to make themselves into martyrs rather than to actually get caught up or ahead with work. For whatever reason, they do not feel good about what they accomplished during the workweek, so they feel they "deserve" to work on Saturday. And then Saturday is spent daydreaming, organizing and promising oneself to get it together next week. Sound familiar?

Even for some of the most diligent planners, weekend work usually is the result of poor planning, or at least, the wrong type of planning. People wake up Monday morning, head to the office, and immediately make a list of myriad things they need to accomplish that day. Things like paying bills, going to the gym, stopping by the grocery store are all mixed in with actual work tasks and personal bailout planning. Come 5:00 pm, many items are crossed off the list, some get pushed back until tomorrow, and a new list gets created for the next day.

To-do lists are great tools, but this type of daily list may do more harm than good. Listing everything and the kitchen sink to accomplish each day creates a lot of busywork and gives all tasks, important and non-important, equal weight. In other words, there is lots of motion, but not necessarily much action.

A better way to plan is to create a list of *weekly* goals, no more than a handful of critical items you need to take action on in a given week, and keep this list close at hand during your workweek. We recommend creating your list on Sunday nights, because you can spend an hour (tops) without distraction and interruption.

Most of us greatly overestimate the number of things we can accomplish on a given day, but greatly underestimate what we can accomplish during a full week.

Stick to a few big action items and hold yourself accountable. If you need to keep a daily reminder list of things to do, that's fine. But don't confuse the motions of doing laundry or stopping at the drugstore as action items that move the ball forward. You can cross off hundreds of these "accomplishments" each week from your list and still feel you did not get anything done. Then you are right back at the office on yet another Saturday morning.

Plan your week, not your day. Focus on the truly important, not the immediate, the action, not the motion. And come to work Monday morning with your week's plan in hand. Sunday night is a great night for weekly planning. Your Saturdays will thank you for it.

Bailout and Beyond Tip #3
Timing is Telling

In our society of hurry up, with mobile phones, instant messaging, social networking where we can follow most everyone at any time, and wireless everything, it seems like there would be no miscommunication regarding time. But there still is…often, and without much thought for the person waiting.

The time to let someone know you are behind schedule, running late, or stopping to do something before seeing him or her, is long before the scheduled time.

Let's say that you have a 9:30 AM meeting an hour away from your home or office, and it is currently 8:45 AM. Here are your choices:

A) Hop in the car and crank the tunes…what are fifteen minutes anyway?

B) Touch up your hair and check your clothes because if you are going to be tardy, you might as well look fabulous upon entry.

C) Start thinking of excuses!

D) Get in the car and start driving really fast…maybe you can make it and not get a ticket. Cross your fingers for all green lights!

E) Contact the person with whom you are meeting or the office where you are expected immediately.

Own the accountability by:

1)   Requesting the person please forgive you.

2)   Simply state you made a mistake, and you are running 15 minutes behind.

3)   Ask if the meeting can please still take place.

Hopefully you chose E! With that smart choice, reflect on what you usually do...is the answer still E? Part of the answer in E is that you do not make excuses or provide your history, or delve into your "back story". This other person should not have to listen to that while rearranging something and/or accommodating you.

The primary reason for acting on choice E is that it shows courtesy toward the other person. It tells that person you are thinking of him or her...and not just you!

Perhaps that individual or office team can get something else done in those 15 minutes. An errand can be run, a note written, a story read, etc., and with that warning, so to speak, the other person has the option about his or her time. Without that warning, you are basically proving that you think your time is more valuable than the other person.

Another reason for following through on E is that you are calm and focused and less likely to make frantic driving decisions or cause situations for others on your path.

Timing is telling with respect to availability, and in this case, disposition and respect. Remember that the next time you are running late…and act on the knowledge that the E answer provides you. No excuses, rather ownership of your actions, and planning ahead will keep you from needing a mini bailout for those times!

Activity: Availability...Your Own Time Parameters

Even with proper planning, it still may often seem like time keeps getting away from you or that there just are not enough hours in the day for everything you need to accomplish.

Imagine if you set a plan for your days including sleep time, preparation time, driving/commuting time, time for goals, working out, meals and family. You may be surprised by how much actual time is available in those 24 hours we have available each day.

This next activity is brief and takes only a bit of your time, but after completing it, you may seemingly have more time to spare!

The idea is to start at the top of the chart by listing how much time you want to allocate to various tasks each day, and then calculate how much time remains for work.

Because time is a non-renewable resource, decide how much time you want to spend on yourself, or with your family and friends *before* thinking about your workday. Establish these parameters on your time and your family and friends' time and, of equal importance, communicate these parameters to those affected. Your friends and family will learn to respect your time (they may even follow your example.)

We save work for last because *you are so much more than what you do for a living.* You want to work to live and not live to work, so keep work last. Once you account for non-work availability, when you are at work you will be much more dedicated to that sole time and focus, and not be distracted with thoughts of "making time" for yourself and others. Your work productivity, and therefore, your results, should rise accordingly.

Here's the form for what we call "Availability":

Availability

Want		**Do**	
Activity	**24**	**Activity**	**24**
Sleep	_____	Sleep	_____
Family	_____	Family	_____
Downtime	_____	Downtime	_____
Prep., Travel & Meals	_____	Prep., Travel & Meals	_____
Workout	_____	Workout	_____
Goals	_____	Goals	_____
Other	_____	Other	_____
Work	_____	Work	_____

Sleep is how much time you spend in non-awake hours either actually sleeping or resting in a prone position (not too complicated, right?).

Family is the time you spend with friends and family; whether that is on-line, on the phone, writing to them, or in person.

Downtime is non-value added time, such as surfing the web, watching TV, reading a magazine for fun, or just being alone.

Prep, Travel & Meals accounts for the time you spend getting yourself and others ready, as well as time in transport to and from places and meals alone or with others.

Workout is whatever you do to stay fit and healthy. This ranges from yoga to weights to walking or running or swimming…and all things in between.

Goals encompass things that you are working toward. Time spent on this book is *Goals* time. Additionally, if you have a goal to learn a language, that would be in goals. Some people even place meditation in *Goals*, since meditation may not be considered *Downtime* or a *Workout*.

Other is anything that was not accounted for earlier. Perhaps you are in a play, or tutoring someone, and you do not consider those *Goals* or *Work*, you would put that time in *Other*.

Work is last for the reasons stated at the start of this activity. Work should follow everything else, and in effect, account for the time that is left over after all the other areas are satisfied. Live your life fully, and let work flow differently than you may typically see it. Far too often people think, think, think about work, work, work, and say or believe they cannot do the other things, but when you prioritize your time, your ideals will likely change.

Track this each day for a week and make adjustments from the want based on the do, and vice versa. You will see and feel your attitude and your actions change pretty quickly. Minimally, after 21-28 days, you may very well have a fully renewed appreciation and respect for *your* time.

Remember, we all have the same amount of time in a day...it is what we CHOOSE to do with that time that makes the difference in creating a successful bailout plan. Make time for action, not motion.

Activity: Selections and Values

In order to ensure you do not move away from what is primarily important to you and your life in creating your bailout plan, please read the following list of descriptive words and/or values.

The following 52 words mean different things to different people. *Read them for what they mean to you.* Because Selections and Values is about *your selections*, and *your values* based on *your life*, our definitions for the words need not be given, for the definitions may create bias.

After reading the comprehensive list, underline the eight that resonate most with you for either what is in your life or what you are striving to achieve.

Variety	Community	Structure	Belief
Frivolity	Kinship	Abundance	Opportunity
Intensity	Recognition	Progress	Possibility
Reward	Advancement	Family	Hope
Challenge	Accomplishment	Fun	Freedom
Balance	Understanding	Change	Risk
Chaos	Consistency	Status	Pride
Happiness	Showmanship	Friends	Joy
Respect	Sportsmanship	Character	Adventure
Fair	Flexibility	Kindness	Esteem
Conflict	Willingness	Integrity	Longevity

Of those eight, circle the four that are more important to you than the other four. Lastly, star your top two.

Keep those top two words, your most important Values and Selections, in mind throughout the entire book and your personal bailout plan to make certain you do not attempt to do anything that does conflicts or runs counter to your Values and Selections.

In order to ensure you are clear on your values, and that you can articulate them later, record your top two values below. Create a definition to which you can refer back to when finalizing your own bailout plan and keep your perspective on what is most important to you.

Value 1: _____

Definition:

_____

_____

_____

Value 2: _____

Definition:

_____

_____

_____

Here is an example for you to use as a guide:

Selections and Values

Variety	Community	Structure	(Belief)
Frivolity	Kinship	Abundance	Opportunity
Intensity	Recognition	Progress	Possibility
Reward	Advancement	(Family)	Hope
Challenge	Accomplishment	Fun	Freedom
Balance	Understanding	Change	Risk
Chaos	Consistency	Status	Pride
(Happiness)	Showmanship	Friends	Joy
Respect	Sportsmanship	Character	Adventure
Fair	Flexibility	Kindness	Esteem
Conflict	Willingness	(Integrity)	Longevity

Value 1: Integrity

Definition: Knowing what I do is trustworthy, straight-forward and fair.

Value 2: Family

Definition: The friends I choose, and the relatives I have in my life who are part of love and growth.

71

Activity: Assessing Interests…From Exposure to Expertise

Just as you have values that are important to you based on your life's lessons, you have a lot of interests as well. Still, not everyone will have a profitable, positive impact in each area, so it is important to decipher where you are and where you want to be based on your interests. This is a multi-step approach to sorting out your situation in life through your interests, and prioritizing where your focus is most likely suited for you in your bailout plan. This is about discovering your intentional and unintentional preparations, and creating your opportunities based on what you learn.

On the longer, bold lines, record the things that you thoroughly enjoy and can imagine spending more time doing which may also have value to others in some way.

Enjoyable Activities

___ _____ ___ _____ ___ _____

___ _____ ___ _____ ___ _____

___ _____ ___ _____ ___ _____

___ _____ ___ _____ ___ _____

___ _____ ___ _____ ___ _____

Next, go back and note whether you have
Exposure (R), Experience (C), or Expertise (S)
in each area by noting an R, C or S in the small
space to the left of each interest you recorded.
Think of **Exposure (R)** as having been around it
or involved but limited due to time, funds or
interest at the time, **Experience (C)** as having
been involved repeatedly with interest, with a
plan to do more, but limited due to availability
or funds at the time, and **Expertise (S)** as
something you have done a lot and could likely
even teach or share if given an opportunity.

Re-list your interests here by the three options:

Exposure (R)	Experience (C)	Expertise (S)
_____	_____	_____
_____	_____	_____
_____	_____	_____
_____	_____	_____
_____	_____	_____

Take a look at your responses in each category and
decide on your top two to four favorites in each
area, and record them below:

Exposure (R)	Experience (C)	Expertise (S)
_____	_____	_____
_____	_____	_____
_____	_____	_____
_____	_____	_____

Lastly, transfer your responses below and then decide one step, your next step to take that will move you to the next level (for Exposure and Experience) and one step to increase, maintain, or promote yourself (for Expertise.)

Think about what it will take, whether you are interested, and what you are willing to do to advance your position in each interest.

For each Exposure, Experience, and Expertise, commit to when, specifically, you will take that next step:

Exposure (R)	Next Step	When

Experience (C)	Next Step	When

Expertise (S)	Next Step	When

Example of Activities to get to Growth Plan:

Enjoyable Activities

S Math   S Finance   R Teaching
R Speaking   C Coaching   C Partnering
C Crafts   C Biking   S Swimming
S Marketing   R Creativity   R Innovation
S Managing   S Baking   C Gardening

Categorized

Exposure (R)	Experience (C)	Expertise (S)
Teaching	Coaching	Math
Speaking	Partnering	Finance
Creativity	Crafts	Swimming
Innovation	Biking	Marketing
	Gardening	Managing
		Baking

Top 2 - 4

Exposure (R)	Experience (C)	Expertise (S)
Teaching	Coaching	Math
Speaking	Partnering	Finance
Creativity	Crafts	Marketing
Innovation		Managing

The Growth Plan Example:

Growth Plan

Exposure (R)	Next Step	When
Teaching	Volunteering	tuesday
Speaking	Class Schedule	Thursday
Creativity	Group	Today
Innovation	Brainstorming	Next Monday

Experience (C)	Next Step	When
Coaching	Team Schedule	Today
Partnering	Contact List	Tuesday
Crafts	Class Gchedule	Next Tuesday

Expertise (S)	Next Step	When
Math	Tutoring	Next Wednesday
Finance	Tax Classes	Today
Marketing	Outreach to Mktg.	Next Thursday
Managing	Contact HR	Today

Activity: Planned Accomplishments

Remember those strength and opportunity traits you gathered in *Step 1: Assess*? It is time to look back and list your overall top three strength traits, and top three opportunity traits by combining your self-assessment with the feedback provided by trusted colleagues, family or friends.

Go back to pages 48-49, and review your lists. You may find some listings that you can consolidate. For example, if you have kind, considerate, and thoughtful listed separately as strengths, you can combine those traits as "common courtesy", or something else you deem appropriate. Similarly, if you got feedback stating poor punctuality, tardiness and rushing to get things done, you may label that "time stress". Based on your assessing and through the input of others, prioritize your top strengths and opportunities below:

Top strengths:

1. _____

2. _____

3. _____

Top opportunities:

1. _____

2. _____

3. _____

Using these responses, create your own Planned Accomplishments that fully demonstrate the characteristic of each strength and self-improvement for the opportunities.

By our definition, Planned Accomplishments means: Goals + Actions = Results. If you plan to get something done you have a goal, and when you take steps to make it happen, you are acting upon it and in the end, you get your results.

For this exercise, you will focus on both your strength traits as well as your opportunity traits. The reason you will want to do this is so that you do not end up working only on improvements of things that are not your best qualities, and therefore, get discouraged or neglect your strengths.

Additionally, those who continue to hone strengths are forward-focused and are continually learning. This keeps you on track for your Cycle of Self, and out of self-absorbed, self-worship times in your life, where you may be acting selfishly or tending to only your own needs.

While completing this last exercise in *Step 2: Prioritize*, you will want to avoid simply qualifying your responses (for example, if a strength is presentation skills, the Planned Accomplishment would not be "I will do more speaking engagements," or if an opportunity to improve is a short temper, the Planned Accomplishment would not be "I will be more kind"). Instead, take time to really reflect and craft responses that are specific, challenging and carry accountability. For example, just as good leaders decide where Point A and Point

B are, a Planned Accomplishment for the above mentioned strength trait example would be clear and measurable when stated "I will engage in paid speaking engagements minimally once per month with up to three days available for events". Similarly, for the opportunity trait, a well-stated approach could be "I will refrain from snapping at family members for interrupting and be patient with ideas that are not my own when making family decisions". This language allows for an identifiable, attainable Planned Accomplishment.

You may again question the reason for setting an accomplishment for a strength as a strength already has a positive impact on your life. Strength, unfortunately, can fade or become overlooked when one focuses solely on opportunity traits. So in your bailout plan, you are going to utilize both your strengths and your opportunities to best prepare and take full advantage of your opportunities.

Now it's your turn…on the next few pages, note future activities or events that will depict you fully engaging the characteristics. State it in such a way that if the event was being broadcast and you saw yourself, you'd clearly know you were demonstrating what you set out to do. Once you have the act/action, then add the first step to get there and when you will take that step as well. Examples are on pages 82 and 83 for reference.

**Activity: Strength Trait
Planned Accomplishments**

1. Trait: _____

Accomplishment_____

_____

1st Step:_____Day:_____

2. Trait: _____

Accomplishment_____

_____

1st Step:_____Day:_____

3. Trait: _____

Accomplishment_____

_____

1st Step:_____Day:_____

Activity: Opportunity Trait
Planned Accomplishments

1. Trait: _____

Accomplishment_____

_____

1st Step:_____Day:_____

2. Trait: _____

Accomplishment_____

_____

1st Step:_____Day:_____

3. Trait: _____

Accomplishment_____

_____

1st Step:_____Day:_____

Here are the examples for the Strength Traits
Planned Accomplishments:

Strength Trait Planned Accomplishments

1. Trait: Determination

Acomplishment Network in new
environment monthly

1st Step: Read step 4   Day: Thursday

2. Trait: Compassion

Acomplishment Visit Grandparents
monthly

1st Step: Call to Schedule   Day: Tomorrow

3. Trait: Drive

Acomplishment Target groups and
schools to talk finance

1st Step: Block time   Day: Today

Here are the examples for the Opportunities Traits
Planned Accomplishments:

Opportunity Trait Planned Accomplishments

1. Trait: *Punctuality*

Acomplishment *Arrive 10 minutes early at client site*

1st Step: *Leave early*   Day: *Today*

2. Trait: *Blurting*

Acomplishment *Wait until appropriate time in Monday Meetings to ask ?s*

1st Step: *Listen*   Day: *Monday*

3. Trait: *Consideration*

Acomplishment *Share ideas with new team in office*

1st Step: *Contact HR* Day: *Friday*

Jenn Ingallinera – Prioritizing to a Position

Bailout plans are not just for entrepreneurs and the self-employed - those in the corporate world can reap the rewards of a successful bailout plan. Just ask Jenn Ingallinera.

A few years ago Jenn looked into her future and didn't like what she saw. Although she held a good position as a corporate trainer for a large company, Jenn foresaw changes in her work environment that posed significant risks to her livelihood.

"More and more, our corporate training programs were becoming automated or outsourced," said Jenn. "Advances in technology were rendering the more traditional training model obsolete, or able to be conducted off-site and implemented online. I knew that I needed to shift my career to one where my physical presence was irreplaceable by outside forces."

Jenn decided to take things into her own hands.
Jenn decided to prioritize.

Prior to arriving at her present job, Jenn was a
corporate recruiter with another large firm. While
the trend in human resource advancement seemed to
lead from corporate recruiter to corporate trainer,
Jenn thought otherwise. Jenn believed that she
could best position herself as a corporate recruiter
for a Fortune 500 company by emphasizing the
skills she learned from the training side of the
business.

Jenn sought out a position in corporate recruiting
for a Fortune 500 company, and prioritized her skill
sets to best match the qualities sought by that type
of high-level employer.

"I interviewed for recruiting positions and led with
the experience I gained from corporate training,"
said Jenn. "Sure, it helped that I had prior
experience in corporate recruiting, but what really
set me apart from the competition was the way I
positioned myself as someone who could judge
applicants beyond their initial hire. As a former
trainer, I could better understand how a new
employee would learn and grow professionally over
time – how they would respond to training."

Jenn prioritized the attributes and skill sets that
differentiated her from other job seekers and led
with those qualities in her interviews. And as (not!)
luck would have it, Jenn landed that corporate
recruiting position with a Fortune 500 firm in no
time at all.

Looking for a job right now? Make sure you prioritize the attributes that make you unique. Jenn Ingallinera may just recruit *you.*

Step 3: LEVERAGE

"We must develop knowledge optimization initiatives to leverage our key learnings."

~ Scott Adams

Step 3: Leverage

Leverage your preparation to create or expand new opportunities.

Reason*:* *Leverage* is our third step because it incorporates the steps of *Assess* and *Prioritize* and brings them into a light that has even greater value. By *Leveraging* the information from *Assess* and *Prioritize*, you will begin to gain confidence and direction. It is essential to realize what, how and who are involved and the degrees of assistance or separation that exists for your plan to work. When considering using the term *Leverage*, we also thought of position, move and grow, and were clear that leveraging was not manipulating or using. Please be mindful of all of those thoughts. *Leveraging* is part of networking and interacting for a greater good...in this case, your bailout plan.

Activities: Circle of Trust, Life Area Planned Accomplishments.

Up until this point in the book, you've focused mostly on the preparation side of creating your bailout plan. You've assessed where you want to go, and you have prioritized your preparations to make sure you get there.

Now you will begin to shift more toward the creation and expansion of opportunity, and leveraging is the bridge to getting there. A critical step in your bailout plan is to leverage your preparations to create opportunities. While you have searched inside yourself for answers on how to better your preparations, you will want to enlist others to assist you in finding your opportunities.

A main part of your success in this step is to recognize that *leveraging someone is not using or manipulating them*. Rather, leveraging is requesting the input, and recognizing the position, influence and knowledge of someone, and enlisting their support and ideas for your success. Your bias may lead you to those who only see the best in you, or those you have called on before. As in other steps, check your bias, focus on your results to strip out the bias, and stay focused on your bailout plan. This third step blends preparation and opportunity to allow the two to flow into future steps: *Communication* and *Act.*

Opportunity does not knock (on your door). *You have to knock on opportunity's door*! There are a lot of things you can do - they all begin with you. Enlist others along the way in order to move beyond your own sphere of influence while creating your bailout plan.

Bailout and Beyond Tip #4
Get Out There!

When I'm at a loss for creative ideas, I often open up one of my desk drawers and take out my stack of business cards that I've accumulated over years of networking. Some of my contacts are current while others are individuals with whom I have not spoken with for some time. Some people I know well and some people I do not remember. But all of these contacts have one important thing in common.

I never met any of them sitting behind my desk.

I belong to several organizations and every day there are meetings, luncheons, or other types of gatherings. I often weigh my ability to attend a given event against my current workload, and all too often my workload wins. But I've also discovered that I have always come out ahead by leaving my desk and meeting new people, more so than I ever could have by staying put, no matter how much work I have.

When I prepare for a meeting or event, I usually have a specific goal in mind. I want to run into such and such person and ask her about such and such opportunity. Sometimes the plan works - I see the person I want to see and we discuss a specific opportunity that is of mutual interest or benefit.

But other time, things do not go as planned. The person I want to see is not there, we did not get time to speak, or the opportunity I want to discuss no longer exists. And, ironically, these are some of the times I come away from my meeting with great results!

How can that be? Because regardless if the person I seek is at the event, I am prepared just the same. I am free to seek out other opportunities and my opportunity-seeking antenna needs to constantly be turned on.

At any given event you are in front of scores of people with different backgrounds and expertise. Talk to them and learn from them. Leverage their expertise. If you are speaking with Sally the banker, then find out everything you can about banking trends and issues. Do you want to become a banker? Probably not, but who knows what type of ideas arise from the discussion? Perhaps several area banks are closing or consolidating and many top area executives are searching for other jobs or opportunities. Wouldn't their research and opportunity analysis be of interest to you?

Day to day responsibilities and work deadlines often compete for your time against outside professional and civic functions. You must budget your time in advance to force yourself to be available. Block off certain hours and plan your work knowing that you will be out of the office during specific times. If you "play it by ear" and only attend events if you have enough time that day, you will never leave your desk.

Get out there and create your opportunities.

Don't Quit Your Day Job

Everyone knows "Dave." Dave has a well paying job but still feels uneasy about his future. Dave feels the need to create his own bailout plan. Dave assesses what areas of his life he wants to improve, prioritizes activities that make the most positive impact to his bailout plan and Dave leverages others to better take advantage of opportunities. So far, so good.

But then Dave follows the advice of countless get-rich-quick consultants and begins to find ways to quit his job, so that he can devote 100% of his time to implementing his bailout plan or devising additional bailout plans. Dave views his job as an anchor, not as a life raft, and he decides that his goal should be to replace his monthly salary, as soon as possible, with alternative income so he can quit his job and be a full-time opportunity seeker.

Don't be a Dave. Don't quit your job.

Your current job is much more than the cash equivalent of your salary and benefits. Your job affords you the leverage that you need to find and fund your bailout plan opportunities.

The movers and shakers of your community likely belong to several civic, professional or social organizations. Leverage your job in order to place yourself in their circles. By joining organizations as a representative of your company, you will achieve a far greater level of legitimacy than you otherwise would on your own. Plus, memberships and meeting fees add up quickly when they come entirely out of your pocket.

Join civic and professional organizations as a representative of your company, but don't quit leveraging opportunities simply because you are on company time. Your job affords you opportunities to connect with people who you otherwise would not on your own.

Leveraging your job allows you to better leverage your opportunities. Don't be a Dave. Don't quit. Leverage instead.

Leveraging Others' Expertise

In the *Assess*, you reviewed your Life Areas, and in the *Prioritize*, you explored your Exposure, Experience and Expertise. Now, let's expand upon both those exercises by identifying desirable attributes in others, and ways for you to better leverage the expertise of others into your own experiences and expertise.

Keep in mind the feedback you received from 4-10 people during Step 1: *Assess*. It was not long ago that you asked for feedback regarding your strength traits and opportunity traits. By completing the Strengths and Opportunities exercise, you may have already thought about some of the people who you admire, trust and respect. Those same individuals may be called upon here, and throughout your bailout plan, but the people you leverage in this chapter do not need to be those same contacts.

The two activities: Circle of Trust, and Life Area Planned Accomplishments, will involve your ideas and those of others. Additionally, you will be exploring and considering people's backgrounds in order to gain additional feedback so that you can transition from your preparation activities into realizing your opportunities fully. Taking the time and spending the energy in *Leverage* is a readying stage for being effective when you *Communicate* and *Act*.

Bailout and Beyond Tip #5
Adopt and Adapt

It's been said and heard repeatedly that imitation is the most sincere form of flattery. It is even a proverb, yet few of us feel quite that way when someone presents what looks like our work, or appears in the same outfit/suit we have on that day. Often flattery feels like trickery or something not well thought through. What gives? Perhaps Benjamin Franklin said it best when he announced, "There is much difference between imitating a man and counterfeiting him." I happen to agree with the beloved Mr. Franklin, and I suggest the concept of *adopt and adapt*.

Adopt and adapt is when you see, hear, feel, or experience something another person does or says or believes and you consider it, process it, perhaps research it further, and configure it to your situation or style. In other words, first you observe, second, you experience, third, you incorporate, and fourth, you present. I like the fact that Dr. Joyce Brothers said, "Listening, not imitation, may be the sincerest form of flattery," because for me, it is part of that first step of observation. Observation happens fully when all senses are engaged. As simple as a new fashion trend may be, if we partake in it, it is about the look, feel, response, happiness, etc…and that may be just a skinny jean, or wide belt! Imagine what will take place when you are looking at styles, impact, approaches, or philosophies!

How do you give credit where credit is due? "No one ever became great by imitation," according to Samuel Johnson! So how are we great when the world is not spinning off it's axis with truly original ideas? It is that we give 100% credit for direct quotations, full processes, or uses of materials such as articles or books, and we give partial credit for conceptual ideas or summations that are tempered with personal opinion. The reference is for respect and referral for the person first learning of an idea. At no time do we effectively just "borrow" or outright steal ideas, concepts, etc. Still, we have the right to base our opinions/actions on others...it would be difficult not to do so.

Simply put, if we are leaning toward someone's fashion style, or directly copying it, at the least, let the person know personally that s/he inspired you and that they may see a bit of their style in yours and that you appreciate their leading the way and/or introducing you to that look/feel. With work style and efforts, do the same by using expressions like "You stated that well...I am making a note of that" or "Thank you for the insight, I will be incorporating that in my next presentation." What you do not want to do, is watch every gesture, move and nuance and attempt to replicate it...fashion-wise or work-style-wise. Most of us have undoubtedly seen the student attempt to become the teacher by literally masquerading as the teacher. It is not only awkward, but embarrassing for those of us experiencing it right along with the person demonstrating it!

Rule of thumb, you will be a second rate someone else imitator, and you have the ability to consistently be a first-rate you. Keep that in mind, and adopt what you like about an idea/presentation/style, and adapt it to you, and you will continue to be unique and evolving. According to Mahatma Gandhi, "adaptability is not imitation. It means power of resistance and assimilation." I believe you are adaptable, and there is no need for thoughtless or shallow flattery here! So, like a bumper sticker seen somewhere on the highway read *you came into this world an original, don't leave it an imitation*, keep the difference in mind as you leverage things and people all around you for your bailout plan.

Activity: Circle of Trust

Before delving into the Circle of Trust activity, imagine your life, your influences, your memories, and those people who you aspire to be like, or whose guidance you seek. Consider others you look towards for opinions and/or are a part of your everyday life. All the people you have considered have either earned, or not earned, your trust. A Circle of Trust allows you to visually see who is where in terms of trust for you. You are about to determine where each person belongs in your Circle of Trust, so that you can then anticipate how much to share, ask and even expect from each of them.

Use a five-point scale to determine levels of trust. Be straight-forward and not wishful or full of supposition. Go back in your mind and compare interactions with people who you see each day, hear from rarely, and/or give and receive information. As a challenging reminder, keep wishful thinking and bias at bay while completing your Circle of Trust, and use the following levels of trust to guide you:

1) No Trust. Those people that have not earned your trust, lost your trust, or are so new to you that they have not yet been in a position to be trusted.

2) Limited Trust. Those that have earned some trust or have lost some of your trust, or are still new to you but have the potential to be trusted in growing ways.

3) Partial Trust. Those people who have either earned your trust over time, or who have faded in your level of trust because of past disappointments. The *trust jury* may still be out on these people.

4) Intimate Trust. These people have earned your trust. You have decided that these people are to be trusted with ideas and details that you may not wish to share with many others.

5) Complete Trust. These few people have fully earned your trust. These people share many experiences with you or one particular situation where a special bond was formed. This complete level of trust is shared, and you know many things about one another that others do not know, and/or have not been trusted to honor and protect.

Here's an example:

Name	Level of Trust	Reason
Ken	1	new in life
Brother	5	Knowsall - confidant
Sister	2	Talks/tells all
Spouse	5	Best friend + confidant
Dad	3	Limited communication
Mom	4	Makes time/interested
Sue	4	Shared stories/Doesit bbl
Sarah	2	Only shared a few things

The space below provides you the opportunity to consider your contacts and your level of trust:

Name	Level of Trust	Reason
_____	_____	_____
_____	_____	_____
_____	_____	_____
_____	_____	_____
_____	_____	_____
_____	_____	_____
_____	_____	_____
_____	_____	_____
_____	_____	_____
_____	_____	_____
_____	_____	_____
_____	_____	_____
_____	_____	_____

Now take your list of people and arrange them on your Circle of Trust. People in all rings can and may move, so be prepared to review this often. For your bailout plan, consider how to leverage people based on your level of trust. It is important to reiterate the fact that *we are not suggesting taking advantage of, or manipulating, anyone.* Let go of your bias, or baggage, and be clear, direct and reciprocate when looking to leverage other's positions and perspectives.

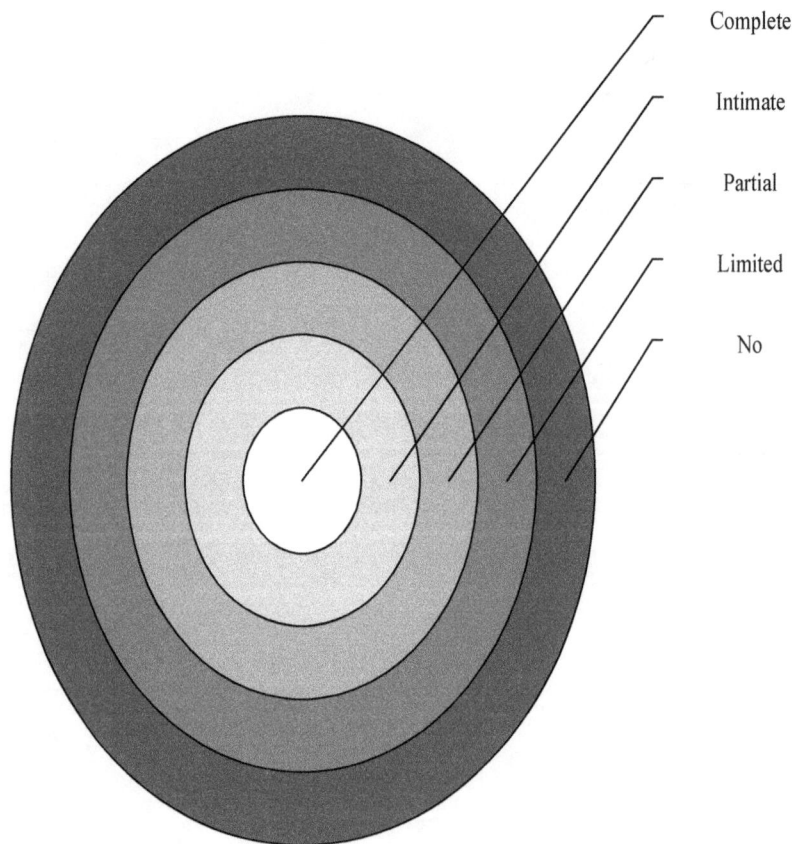

Complete

Intimate

Partial

Limited

No

You may have a greater number of people in your Circle of Trust list and, therefore, listed in your circle on the previous page. As an example, here is how the list used earlier transferred to the Circle of Trust:

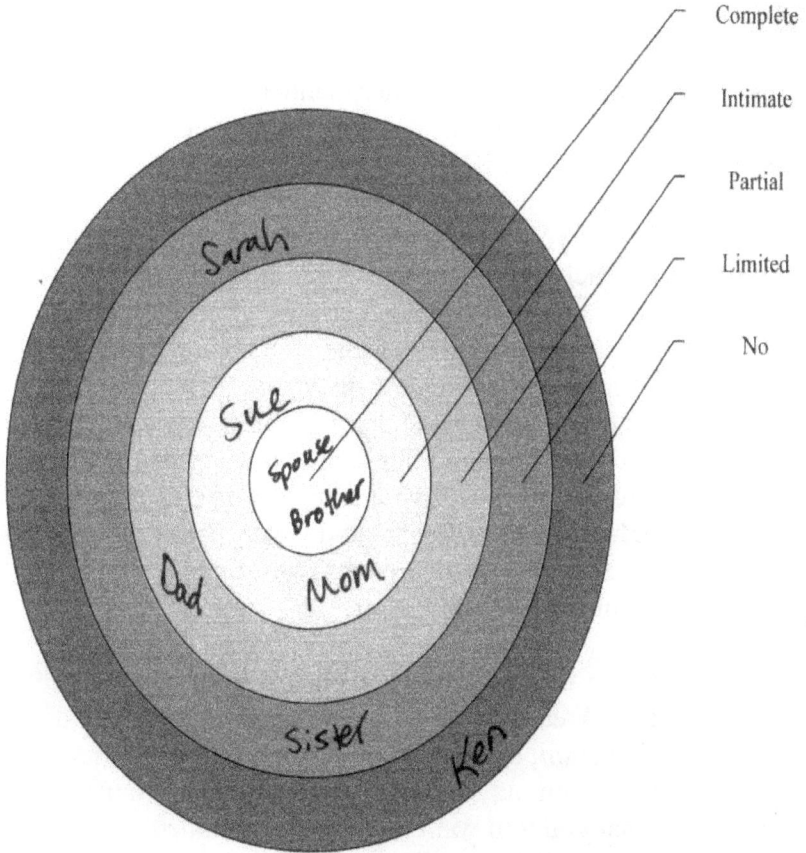

Activity: Life Area Planned Accomplishments

Equipped with a better understanding of the levels of trust you have for the people in your life, now shift gears momentarily and return back to one of the first activities, the Life Area Review.

Work below to identify Planned Accomplishments that will position you to best leverage the expertise of those you have either identified in your Circle of Trust, or will consider once you are done with completing Life Area Planned Accomplishments.

Just as you established Planned Accomplishments for each of your strength and opportunity traits, you will now set bigger, loftier plans for the three Life Areas you wish to address.   Take a look back at your Life Area Review on page 43, and determine the areas of your life upon which you wish to focus your bailout plan. These are typically your Life Area where you have the biggest discrepancy between where you are and where you want to be, but they may just be your lowest three numbers…it's up to you.

In our example, we have chosen to focus upon the Life Areas of *Career/Work*, *Communication* and *Direction*, because these Life Areas scored the lowest on our 5-point scale. Here is an example of what you will want to do for the Planned Accomplishments for your Life Areas:

Life Area Planned Accomplishments

1. Life Area: Career/Work

Accomplishment: Have updated resume and bio completed

1st Step: Print existing resume Day: Tuesday

2. Life Area: Communication

Accomplishment: Remain open to Constructive Criticism

1st Step: Ask for feedback Day: Thursday

3. Life Area: Direction

Accomplishment: Decide how my strengths + opportunities relate to my role

1st Step: Review feedback Day: Friday

Move to the next page for yours.

Activity: Life Area Planned Accomplishments

1. Life Area: _____

Accomplishment: _____

_____

1st Step: _____ Day: _____

2. Life Area: _____

Accomplishment: _____

_____

1st Step: _____ Day: _____

3. Life Area: _____

Accomplishment: _____

_____

1st Step: _____ Day: _____

This is a perfect time to take your Life Area Planned Accomplishments one step further! For your first, second and third Life Areas of importance, think of people you know who can potentially assist you in achieving your goals and Planned Accomplishments.

While you may know a lot of people, you will want to focus on those included in your Circle of Trust, or who have areas of experience or expertise you admire or aspire to emulate.

You may experience a win for both you and each of your peers by working together to achieve your Planned Accomplishment. Many people receive a great deal of personal satisfaction assisting others and will benefit from this exercise just as much as you. In other cases, you may want to respect others' professions and consider paying for, or exchanging services for, their specific opinions or input.

Make sure to share with each contact:

- What you admire about him or her.
- What you perceive as their areas of expertise.
- What you would like to learn from him or her.
- How you believe they can help you reach your success.

The following page is an example for one Life Area. Again, prioritize your most urgent Life Areas, which are typically those where you rated yourself the lowest score on the five-point scale, or have the biggest gap, in current scores compared to your desired number. After you review the example, please complete your own exercises specific to your bailout plan:

Life Area #1 _Career/Work_

Planned Accomplishment #1 _Get in a position to be considered for advancement._

Contact In Life Area	Experience/ Expertise	Assistance to Request
Mgr.-Sue	Company	Feedback
HR-Gary	Company	Next Steps
Tom	Resumes	Review
Carol	Leadership	Feedback
Sydney	Career Coach	Presenting Me
Laura	Sales	Ideas on Selling
Brett	Networking	How/Where
Tom	Industry	Competition
Mark	Industry	Demands

108

Go back to *Step 1: Assess*, on page 42 or page 43 for your Life Areas that you choose for further focus:

Life Area #1_____

Planned Accomplishment #1_____

_____

Contact In Life Area	Experience/ Expertise	Relation to goal
_____	_____	_____
_____	_____	_____
_____	_____	_____
_____	_____	_____
_____	_____	_____
_____	_____	_____
_____	_____	_____
_____	_____	_____
_____	_____	_____

Life Area #2_____

Planned Accomplishment #2_____

_____

Contact In Life Area	Experience/ Expertise	Relation to goal
_____	_____	_____
_____	_____	_____
_____	_____	_____
_____	_____	_____
_____	_____	_____
_____	_____	_____
_____	_____	_____
_____	_____	_____
_____	_____	_____

Life Area #3_____

Planned Accomplishment #3_____

_____

Contact In Life Area	Experience/ Expertise	Relation to goal
_____	_____	_____
_____	_____	_____
_____	_____	_____
_____	_____	_____
_____	_____	_____
_____	_____	_____
_____	_____	_____
_____	_____	_____

Bailout and Beyond Tip #6
Read the Newspaper

What if a low cost publication existed that was full of local and regional bailout plan opportunities? It not only described trends and opportunities, but people and organizations to contact. What if it was updated daily? This would be a valuable tool to say the least, a "must-have" for the person who seeks to position themselves for greater opportunity. And what if it was delivered to your doorstep, computer, or other electronic device each and every morning?

Your daily newspaper is perhaps the most cost-effective, convenient and comprehensive source of opportunity that you will find. It is packed with information about industry-wide challenges, company-specific opportunities, profiles of community leaders, upcoming community, business and civic events and much more. I have added seven figure clients by reading the newspaper and connecting the dots. I identify public sector challenges, learn about the people or organizations involved, position myself as an expert in helping these organizations overcome these challenges, then pick up the phone or get out pen and paper and make contact. It is really that straight-forward.

You want to meet the movers and shakers in the community? Your newspaper's business section likely has a weekly update of local business leaders who have accepted new positions or received a promotion or accolade. Another weekly column usually lists new businesses and/or bankruptcies. Find an opportunity that interests you, research the people who are involved in this arena, and then put yourself out there. If you cannot find a networking opportunity in the newspaper for your topic of interest, keep searching. Use online tools to find similar groups and organizations, and ask around, too.

And don't believe for one second that if a good idea arises from a newspaper article that someone else has already though of it first. Even if you are not the first person to discover an opportunity, you are likely the first person to act upon it. And the bigger or more obvious the opportunity, even the more likely you are the first to pull the trigger. Think of the best looking man or woman at the dance. No one approaches them because they are intimidated, and they assume they have been already been approached by better looking, more accomplished suitors. But often the opposite is true. No one approaches them at all because everyone gives the competition too much credit. Then one brave soul makes the move and the rest of us wind up wondering what just happened.

Your newspaper is your daily guide map of opportunity. Read your paper today with your opportunity antenna fully extended. What are the opportunities and challenges in your community? Who are the key people? How can I connect the dots?

Then go put yourself out there. The prettiest girl at the dance might just be waiting for someone to finally say hello.

Sean Winton – Fairways to Heaven Golf

To many, golf is much more passion than recreation. Embracing this belief that "it's more than just a game," Scottish-born Sean Winton founded Fairways to Heaven Golf (http://www.f2hgolf.com) in 1996, and since then, he has offered premium custom golf travel to high net worth individuals, major corporations and golf enthusiasts worldwide.

Whether you want to squeeze in a few rounds while vacationing in the U.S. or you wish to tee it up at the pinnacle of golf destinations, the Old Course at St. Andrew's, Scotland, Sean and Fairways to Heaven Golf can provide exclusive access to major golf course, travel and resort destinations throughout the world.

While Sean has successfully branded Fairways to Heaven Golf as a top golf travel service, recent economic and technological challenges have necessitated some significant changes in the direction of the company. "Over the last few years, consumers have become more and more savvy and comfortable booking golf travel by themselves over the Internet," says Sean. "And in 2008, we've seen overseas golf travel drop off significantly due to the global economic slowdown and very unfavorable exchange rates for foreign currencies versus the dollar. We realized that in order to keep growing, Fairways to Heaven Golf needed to better leverage our integral relationships with golf and resort destinations. We needed to become as equally value added to the destination as we are to the consumer."

Sean began to leverage his proprietary database of customers and golfers as a tool to better market destinations to consumers. Fairways to Heaven has expanded its mission to help resorts and golf courses find golf travelers, while continuing its core practice of helping golf travelers find resorts and golf courses.

"By leveraging our expert knowledge of the golf traveler and what unique and memorable golf experiences he or she demands, we have been able to expand our offerings and create more value for both the golf traveler and the destination host. We've become a full-service golf destination marketing service, and we are uniquely positioned to grow and excel in years to come."

Sean was able to build upon his core business and leverage his preparation to create and expand new opportunities.

Looks like nothing but blue skies and birdies for Fairways to Heaven Golf in the years to come.

Step 4: COMMUNICATE

"Your ability to communicate is an important tool in your pursuit of your goals, whether it is with your family, your co-workers or your clients and customers."

~ Les Brown

Section 4: Communicate

Communicate is seeking out opportunity and asking others to assist you in accomplishing your bailout plan.

Reason: *Communicate* is the fourth step in regaining control of your life is for timeliness and effect. Sure, you will share ideas and talk with others throughout each of the five steps, but once you have completed *Assess, Prioritize,* and *Leverage,* you are in a sound position to *Communicate* clearly and effectively your plan and your approach. We thought about using the term share or the word tell, but the concept of *Communicate* reminds us that there is a give and take with your colleagues, friends and family. You are looking for support and ideas as well. *Communicate* covers all aspects of sharing and telling. It keeps the audience in mind and positions you professionally for your revealing of your plan. *Communicate* is sharing with others and allowing others to share with you.

Activities: 30-Second Pitch, NETWORK Commitment Sheet.

As in Real Estate, where the three most important criteria are said to be location, location, location, the success of your bailout hinges on effective communication, communication, communication!

It is not enough for you to just leverage the expertise of others. If you want to give your bailout plan the greatest probability for success, you will need to leverage the help of others as well. By communicating your bailout plan to others, you enlist others to assist you create or find the opportunities you seek.

Imagine you invented a product that you would like to sell on a mass scale. How would you tell potential buyers about the product? You'd advertise and market, that's how. If you didn't do this, no one would know about your product and you wouldn't sell a thing.

Now imagine you are focused on establishing your bailout plan (we are anticipating you are!). Sure you could go it alone, but for what reason would you? If you advertise and market your dreams by communicating them to others and enlisting their help in creating or finding opportunities for you, you will enjoy a much higher probability of achieving success.

Most of us have no problem promoting a product or service, but we hesitate to promote ourselves or our bailout plans. Perhaps due to fear of rejection or perhaps due to shyness, we keep our dreams and our bailout plans to ourselves. Don't make this mistake! No one says "no" until you ask him or her to say "yes", and they often actually say "yes"!

Communicate your bailout plans to others so they can be a part of your success plan.

Communication also involves listening and being aware of ideas and opportunities. As we discussed in the previous chapters, ideas and opportunities are often abound, but you need to go find them. They won't just come to you. People are the bridge between you and ideas, between your preparation and your opportunity.

While most people attend networking events, not all people effectively communicate. People and communication come together in the form of effective networking. Network with the goal of sharing your bailout plans. Listen to others, be prepared, and consistently be ready to seize an opportunity.

Opportunity awaits – go communicate!

Memorability…It's Up to You

What makes some things, some people or some events more memorable than others? Are they more graphic, louder or more extravagant, or is there some other explanation?

Consider that when people do not remember your name, it is not entirely because they are *bad with names* (which is an overly used and overly accepted excuse for not recalling names). Rather it is likely a combination of their self-interest or disinterest, and your lack of memorability. In order to be memorable, you need to work at being memorable!

What do we mean by memorable? Extreme occurrences, both good and bad, are remembered most. Pause to reflect for 30-60 seconds and recall something tremendously wonderful and then something that nears disgust. Your charge going forward is to make sure the impressions you make on others are closer to the former, rather than the latter experience! When communicating with others, a few simple actions taken on your part can make the difference regarding how you are remembered.

Begin with your approach - smile at the other person. The most common response to a smile is one in kind. As you state your name, say it like the other person has never said it (remember, they have not) - meaning directly and informatively.

Use a red/yellow/green approach to communication. Think stop (red) before saying your name, proceed slowly (yellow), give time and breath after your first name, and then go (green) ahead with your last name. Make the time and effort to connect with names. When it is not your turn to speak, rather than think internally "wow, I did that just right", or "hmmmm…what will I say next?", just listen, as the person with whom you are interacting is saying his or her name. If you are consumed with self-praise, you are likely to miss the other person's name.

Stating your name clearly is only one part of being memorable - remembering the other person's name is of equal importance. Often people will reply that they like someone who they do not know well simply because that person has called him or her by their name. Repeating the other person's name three times assists in your recall. Writing down the person's name is helpful, but the most important part of remembering a name is actually hearing it in the first place! Listening is a key component of communication.

Once you have asked a person's name (and listened to their answer!) resist asking them next about what they "do" for a living. If memorability is your goal, try asking a question that sparks enthusiasm or excitement such as, "What keeps your attention when you are not at work?" or "What do you like to do in your free time?" When people start describing their areas of enjoyment and passion they begin to engage in much more enriching conversation. They will associate that good feeling with you…making you much more memorable to them!

Becoming memorable centers on sincerity and displaying a genuine interest in others. It involves listening as much as speaking. The next time someone fails to remember your name, reflect on how memorable you are and how you may improve. Memorability creates more effective and genuine communication, and better communication allows others to help you with your bailout plan.

The Time to Network is Now

People do a lot of networking when they "need a job", don't they? People consistently say they "have a job, so they don't *need* to network", or worse yet, they *don't have time* to network".

The time to network is now. Networking will be discussed in depth, with steps and plans, but before any of our ideas will resonate with you, you have to decide to network now…not because you *have* to network, but because you *want* to network. What, you say you don't like to network and don't want to? Well then, think about the results of networking and decide you *want the results*. For this, and other things, too, if you shift from the task to the results, you will see your attitude change!

There are not only set times for networking or set places, as networking opportunities are all around you. Imagine every day is one of the first days where you moved to a new location or a new position. Remember how you outreached to people, met them, and how your relationships grew? That was networking, but you perhaps just thought it was "learning the ropes" or meeting people. What you did with those relationships created networks of people…business or personal contacts.

So in progressing through the book, and creating your own bailout, remember if you are wondering if it is a good time to network, it is! The time to network is now!

Activity: 30 Second Pitch

Before you can communicate effectively, you must be certain of what you want to say, how you say it and be determined that your entire message gets conveyed. The old adage 'you never get a second chance to make a first impression' rings true in so many ways. It has been stated that people make a decision about us within as few as 2 seconds up to as many as 30 seconds.

The first impression you make upon another is just that…the first. From there, you have the audience of one or more either interested, engaged, disgusted, or disinterested people, or an array of other things. A 30 Second Pitch is something from you, about you, for sharing quickly and conveniently to convey a message of interest to others in order to keep the conversation moving forward. Your 30 Second Pitch is both your first and *lasting* impression!

What makes this important? All the preparation in the world to share a lot of information about you will not pay off if you are only provided with a small window of time in which to share. A large window of time will be wasted if the first 30 seconds are not utilized fully. We recommend you communicate quickly and effectively something that will leave a good impression, and represents you well. In order to do this, you will first want to decide what you want to communicate.   The following eight questions will serve you well:

1 - What is the other person's interest/offer? This means the other person's area of expertise or desired area of expertise. You must consider your audience of one or more before ever pitching "you."

2 - What enhancement/solution do I bring? Ideas you can communicate towards the other person's interests/offers.

3 - At what am I expert? Go back to your 2-4 areas of expertise and identify what expertise you are communicating and to whom.

4 - What are the needs? What need does the other person have, and what do I need/want from him or her in return?

5 - What makes me unique? Go back to your Strength Areas and Cycle of Self in order to articulate your approach to others.

6 - What are my typical results? Give concrete details. If you are great at investing, share the rate of return. If you are focused, but have difficulty shedding pounds, share your story of results from something else that yielded results.

7 - What will I give right now? What can you leave the person with as a good impression and something of value to him or her…a phone number, a name, an idea, etc. As we will touch on in networking, while you want to get something, you are best served to initially make it about the other person and give a firm, sincere commitment for follow through and providing value.

8 - How will I follow up later? What is one step you will do and when?

You have a form on the next pages for you to create *your* 30 Second Pitch based on these eight questions. After all, when you make or seek an opportunity, you must be prepared!

Here's an example:

30 Second Pitch

Life Area: Financial Date: 3/18

Targeted Person/Audience: Personal Investors w/ online success

What is the other person's interest/offer? Money | Investing

What enhancement/solution do I bring? Money to invest + an interest in an investment club.

At what am I expert? Technology, Systems, Process

What is my need? Being taught on-line investments

What makes me unique? Thorough, risk-taker, Kind

What are my typical results? 98%+ implementation success + 98.5% Return on Investment

What will I give right now? Program reference for speeding up system. Idea for system change.

How will I follow up later? Contact to review IT systems at no cost.

Bringing it together in a statement or statements:

Since your interests include money + success, and I have a little money to invest as well as an interest in starting an investment club, perhaps we can work together. With my expertise in technology, risk-taking comfort, expertise in systems and process, I am looking for someone to teach me about on-line investments. I'm kind and thorough + have a 98% implementation success. I'd like to get similar results for investing. I have an idea of how you may be able to speed up your system. Perhaps we can get together for a complimentary review of your system, and you could give me some ideas on trades? I'll follow up this week to set something up with you.

And now, here are your blank forms for you to complete:

30 Second Pitch

Life Area:_____ **Date:**_____

Targeted Person/Audience: _____

What is the other person's interest/offer? _____

What enhancement/solution do I bring? _____

At what am I expert? _____

What is my need? _____

What makes me unique? _____

What are my typical results? _____

What will I give right now? _____

How will I follow up later? _____

Bringing it together in a statement or statements:

_____

_____

_____

_____

_____

30 Second Pitch

Life Area:_____ **Date:**_____

Targeted Person/Audience: _____

What is the other person's interest/offer? _____

What enhancement/solution do I bring? _____

At what am I expert? _____

What is my need? _____

What makes me unique? _____

What are my typical results? _____

What will I give right now? _____

How will I follow up later? _____

Bringing it together in a statement or statements:

_____

_____

_____

_____

_____

30 Second Pitch

Life Area:_____ **Date:**_____

Targeted Person/Audience: _____

What is the other person's interest/offer? _____

What enhancement/solution do I bring? _____

At what am I expert? _____

What is my need? _____

What makes me unique? _____

What are my typical results? _____

What will I give right now? _____

How will I follow up later? _____

Bringing it together in a statement or statements:

_____

_____

_____

_____

_____

_____

Bailout and Beyond Tip #7
The Business Card Exchange

Finally, at an appropriate point in the conversation, should you want to network, maintain a connection, or even build on making a friend, a typical form of sharing information is the business card exchange. Keep your business cards handy. Digging in your suit or bag or wallet to pull out a half-mangled version of a once lovely card may make you memorable...and not in the way this tip is intended.

When you have your card in your hand, put your thumb under it with your fingers on top of it (much like a top and bottom frame) and present it to the other person with the card outstretched toward the other person near the height level of your face. In other words, banish the thumb on the top of your card, waist level pass to their hand. The point of "framing of the card" near your face, or at least not just at hand-shaking level, is to lock in the lasting impression of you and your name with the person receiving it. The other person will see you and associate the card with your name and face. This furthers your memorability beyond your name.

It is likely you will get the other person's card in the flawed way of meekly providing a card in a fashion similar to a Las Vegas dealer distributing playing cards. That is fine...just adjust quickly by holding it out, reading it, and commenting on it so that the other person knows you took the time to remember him or her. (Think back to how many times you or someone else did not read a business card...it is awkward and a bit of a let down to an otherwise often good experience.) Place the card in a holder, or in the same place from which you retrieved your card to show the importance of the card to you.

Keep in mind, too, it's great to give a card properly and even better to give two…one for the person to keep, and one for the new acquaintance to share with someone else who may be of interest to you. Imagine if you did the same in return with cards and asked for two from each person. Watch when you share the reasoning that you would like the chance to connect that person with someone else via the card – talk about memorable…and lasting!

Networking is a Full-Time, Full-Contact Sport

While there are a lot of suggestions for networking and attending various functions, there are few that we believe serve you best. You will find each of our suggestions are easy to remember, require action on your part and focus more upon the other person than upon yourself.

Just know, networking is not synonymous with communicating. It is your responsibility to make the other person feel connected and interested!

Network by focusing your attention on results and not just the action of being at an event.

Before you use any of the ideas for networking, commit to the following:

1) If you go to a networking event with someone, agree to drive to and from the location together and have minimal (or even no) contact at the event. Having a conversation with your friend while at a networking event just means you wasted time and energy driving to the function when you could have just met where you usually do. If you want time with your buddy, go get a coffee or drink after the networking function; just do not spend your time together since that is not productive!

2) Have enough cards for two per person you can potentially meet. Make sure those cards are up-to-date with no changes in name, email or phone scratched out and written in pen. Is the focus of your bailout plan your career? If so, then get professional cards printed with minimally your

name, email and phone with your 2-4 areas of professional expertise listed. Make sure your cards are only UV coated on the front so that people can make notes on the back.

3) Have easy access to your cards and place those you receive from others in an equally convenient location. Ladies…no purses at networking events, or at least carry small ones and ensure you do not need to fumble with zippers, etc. when getting your cards. Go for functionality at the events and use your pockets for your card and cardholders.

4) Check your attitude and outside interests at the door. Keep in mind the situation, opportunity and focus, and know that your truly do not get a second chance to make a first impression!

A quick way to remember how to communicate is with the acronym. NETWORK:

N - Names
E - Event
T - Target
W - Work
O - Offer
R - Reach
K - Keep

Now that you have a way to remember the sometimes seemingly daunting experience of networking, here are a few ideas for being successful in a NETWORK:

N - Names – Get names, in advance, of who will be there.

E – Event – Attend for at least one hour or more.

T – Target – Plan to make 3-4 solid contacts per hour.

W – Work – Act as if the event is one that you created – work it.

O – Offer – Decide what ideas or benefits you can provide for others.

R – Reach – Reach out to people afterward.

K – Keep – Keep in touch and keep networking.

NAME: locate the person in charge of the event a few days prior to the date. Ask for a list of attendees. Sometimes these lists will not be disclosed, but it's worth a shot. If you do not get the names, arrive early and review the nametags to come up with a plan for who you would like to meet. For your name, wear a name tag. Go ahead and have one made so that you are comfortable with it.

EVENT: No matter how long the networking event lasts, commit to attending minimally for an hour. When people "blow in" and "blow out", others notice. Additionally, staying at least one hour gives you the opportunity to catch latecomers. You already arrived early to see the names and prepare for whom you wish to meet. Now you are poised as the person whom others wish to meet.

TARGET: Target people or companies when you arrive early and plan for whom you want to interact. Target 3-4 solid connections for each hour you are at the engagement. This does not mean you can only speak with 3-4 people, but focus on quality over quantity. Collecting business cards is one thing…getting the perhaps few cards of people who can help further your bailout plan is another. This is communicating versus networking.

WORK: Work the room. Yes, *work it*! This is where you take on the role of a host or co-host. This is not to say you take credit for the event or the party, rather you make it a point to welcome others and introduce them with a firm, quick handshake of 2-4 pumps of the hand, and interested, interactive conversation. When you *appear* as the person to meet, you *become* the person to meet.

OFFER: Even though you are looking to advance in your area(s) of life focus and move forward with your bailout plan at each networking event you attend, make sure you devote equal time and attention to listening to and learning about the other people you meet. They may also have areas of life focus and bailout plans, and good communication is a two-way street. If your expertise can help someone else with their bailout plan, they will be much more likely to help you with yours. Make an offer to follow through with information, a contact or something else, and you will endear yourself to that person. When you follow up with him or her in the future, you are now a welcomed call, e-mail or letter coming across his or her desk, rather than another person just looking for a favor. This is a value position that must be sincere in the offer and quick in the execution.

REACH: You have made the new contact and figured out a value-added connection you can provide. Now be sure to reach back out to him or her after the event. Typically, a follow through outreach within 24 hours is optimal. Keep in mind, a phone call can appear pushy, and an e-mail can be impersonal. Contrarily, a handwritten note is quite personal, and a note with a relevant article or bit of information is a real connection (if you have agreed to follow up via phone or email do that, but if there is no commitment, go for the personal note). Think about it...how many people display, or even save, phone messages or emails? Not many. However, many of us keep handwritten notes as keepsakes because they create a personal connection.

KEEP: It has been stated that you must network regularly...not just when you need something. Networking is a function that you must constantly keep on your weekly to-do lists, not just something to do if you need a new job or referral. Keep also stands for keeping in touch and keeping your word. When a person says he or she will be somewhere or do something on a particular date and then lets it slide, this becomes memorable for all the wrong reasons. Keeping up with your commitments keeps progress on your bailout plan going in the right direction!

Identify three upcoming networking events to attend. Your goal is to create a communication plan in advance of each event. Think about how you will communicate your bailout plan to others, offer your expertise to others to leverage, and finally follow up with new contacts. Use the Network Commitment Sheets to create your NETWORK approach as part of your overall bailout plan.

Activity: Network Commitment Sheet:

Event: **FITNN**   Date: **4/1**

Time: **7:00pm**   Location: **Center G+CC**

Life Area: **Financial**   30-Second Pitch Done ✓

N – Names
**Carol T.   Susan P.   Scott Z.
Steve R.   Tom R.   Debra P.
Matt P.   Stephen Q.**

E – Event   When to arrive: **6:45 pm**

T – Target   Companies/Industries: **Financial**

W – Work   Approach to greeting: **Introduce + ask about FITNN**

O – Offer   General offer: **Review of system**

R – Reach   When will I outreach: **W/in next week**

K – Keep   How will I keep in touch: **Note w/ info.**

After the event, comment on the following result:

N – Names   Who was there: **all but Tom R.**

E – Event   When arrived: **6:45 pm**

T – Target   Who targeted: **Financial – Good Oppty**

W – Work   How well worked: **Met 4 of Targets W/ in 1st hour.**

O – Offer   Specific offer(s): **Carol, Susan, Stephen, Scott to set up review**

R – Reach   When I will outreach: **w/in 2 days**

K – Keep   How will I keep in touch: **Mail w/email follow up**
When: **tomorrow to mail Friday to email**

NETWORK Commitment #1

Event:_____ **Date:**_____

Time: _____ **Location:** _____

Life Area: _____ **30 Second Pitch Done**___

N – Names

_____   _____   _____
_____   _____   _____
_____   _____   _____

E – Event   When to arrive:_____

T – Target   Companies/Industries: _____

W – Work   Approach to greeting: _____

O – Offer   General offer: _____

R – Reach   When will I outreach: _____

K – Keep   How will I keep in touch: _____

After the event, comment on the following result:

N – Names   Who was there: _____

E – Event   When arrived:_____

T – Target   Who targeted: _____

W – Work   How well worked: _____

O – Offer   Specific offer(s): _____

R – Reach   When I will outreach: _____

K – Keep   How will I keep in touch: _____

                When: _____

NETWORK Commitment #2

Event:_____ **Date:**_____

Time: _____ **Location:** _____

Life Area: _____ **30 Second Pitch Done**___

N – Names

_____   _____   _____
_____   _____   _____
_____   _____   _____

E – Event   When to arrive:_____

T – Target   Companies/Industries: _____

W – Work   Approach to greeting: _____

O – Offer   General offer: _____

R – Reach   When will I outreach: _____

K – Keep   How will I keep in touch: _____

After the event, comment on the following result:

N – Names   Who was there: _____

E – Event   When arrived:_____

T – Target   Who targeted: _____

W – Work   How well worked: _____

O – Offer   Specific offer(s): _____

R – Reach   When I will outreach: _____

K – Keep   How will I keep in touch: _____

                When: _____

NETWORK Commitment #3

Event:_____ **Date:**_____

Time: _____ **Location:** _____

Life Area: _____ **30 Second Pitch Done**___

N – Names

_____ _____ _____
_____ _____ _____
_____ _____ _____

E – Event   When to arrive:_____

T – Target   Companies/Industries: _____

W – Work   Approach to greeting: _____

O – Offer   General offer: _____

R – Reach   When will I outreach: _____

K – Keep   How will I keep in touch: _____

After the event, comment on the following result:

N – Names   Who was there: _____

E – Event   When arrived:_____

T – Target   Who targeted: _____

W – Work   How well worked: _____

O – Offer   Specific offer(s): _____

R – Reach   When I will outreach: _____

K – Keep   How will I keep in touch: _____

                 When: _____

Domingo Quintero: The Communicator

The real estate sector was one of the hardest hit in 2008. In many parts of the country, the real estate industry skipped the recession stage and plunged straight into depression. Florida was one of these states. Sales of new and existing homes, and overall home values, saw historical declines.

Only a few short years removed from record real estate agent earnings, 2008 saw many real estate commission earnings plummet faster than home prices. But Domingo Quintero saw his business maintain the same high activity and earning levels that makes him a top producer year in and year out. How did he do it?

Domingo Quintero has friends. Lots of friends in fact.

These days, most people belong to one or more social or business networking sites, such as LinkedIn®, Facebook® or MySpace®. Domingo belongs to them all. And where you or I may have a dozen or so friends and contacts, Domingo has thousands.

"The essence of successful real estate sales is relationship building and constant communication," says Domingo. "I position myself as a valuable informational resource to members of my network."

And very often that information has little or nothing to do with real estate. Many of the hundreds of daily emails that Domingo sends or receives concern area happenings, hard-to-come-by concert or sporting event tickets for sale, or simple personal well-wishes. But each message carries his real estate tagline – a subtle reminder of his profession and availability to help with real estate services when needed.

"I take an anti multi-level marketing approach to sales," says Domingo. "You won't want to avoid me at networking functions because I'm not going to try to push real estate down your throat. Hopefully you'll seek me out at functions because you enjoy receiving my communications and find value in their messages."

Domingo succeeds at real estate, at a time when many others are struggling, because he has mastered the art of communication. Domingo doesn't "sell" real estate – Domingo "sells" Domingo. People want to be in his network because they value his communications, and they want to be his friend.

And when buying or selling real estate, who better
to turn to than a friend? Become friends with
Domingo at http://www.DomingoRealEstate.com.

Step 5: Act

"The great end of life is not knowledge but action."

~ Aldous Huxley

Section 5: Act

You, and you alone, are responsible for creating your own preparation and opportunity. Nobody is going to bail you out, so you must ACT!

Reason: *Act* is the fifth step for creating your bailout plan is that action is imperative for results. Without action the rest of the book is just a bunch of theories and exercises. The difference in your bailout plan being your life's work, or work at this time in your life, is the action you decide to take or not take. We considered calling *Act* do or commit, but ultimately chose *Act* because the word feels concise and real...without action, we just have words. The ideas in the book came from tools and worksheets, and now, the remaining action *is* completely, 100% yours! This is when the plan takes life and becomes your bailout in tandem with your experiences...you *Act* and it is! Remember, Opportunity doesn't knock, you knock on Opportunity's door...

Activities: Bailout Plan 60 Day Calendar, Weekly Reviews.

You have made it through the first four steps of *Hey, Where's My Bailout?* Along the way you have *Assessed* your Life Areas and *Prioritized* these Life Areas and the preparations that increase your probability of success in your Life Areas. You've *Leveraged* your preparation to create more opportunity and you have *Communicated* your bailout plan to others so that they can assist you.

In each chapter, you have completed various activities designed to help you focus on what is really important and unique to *you*, and you have read about others who have implemented the five steps in the creation of their unique, personal bailout plan.

Now it is time to put everything together to finalize your own personal bailout plan.

Step 5: Act is devoted to taking all of the lessons from the first four steps and incorporating them into your bailout plan. All of the previous activities and worksheets can stand on their own, but the summation of these exercises is a roadmap for success – a formula that you can apply to different challenges and situations to create a bailout plan to meet your specific needs, whatever they may be.

Now that you have the tools and knowledge necessary to create your own bailout, the only thing left for you to do is to *Act* upon your plan. This is no small task – rather, it is the most critical component. For various reasons, many people with best intentions fail to act upon their plans and dreams. If they were reading this book, they would create their own bailout plan and then never work to put it into effect. *They are not you, though*, and we don't want this to happen to you! We've created a Bailout Plan 60 Day Calendar that requires you chart your bailout plan action items on a timeline. You will have 60 days to act upon your bailout plan – no more. If you cannot act upon your plan in 60 days, you are unlikely to act on it at all. Your Bailout Plan 60 Day Calendar is designed to hold you accountable to your bailout plan, and ensure that you give yourself the greatest opportunity for success.

We know you will do it! First a few more lessons and a story of inspiration…

Construction Zones Expand Comfort Zones

Commonly people fail to act upon their plans or dreams because they find themselves "outside of their comfort zone."

We like to view a comfort zone best as a construction zone – a place where you have the opportunity to stop traffic, work on things and maintain them…as you deem appropriate. Make your comfort zone into a construction zone by incorporating practices of self-examination (many of them learned from this book) and accepting other perspectives from colleagues (also found here).

People typically become comfortable in routines and procedures, making days and events in our personal and professional lives run smoothly. But with the challenges of today's economy touching almost all industries, it is critical we continue to look at ourselves and what we are doing, in order to recreate, tweak, improve or stretch our current abilities.

Comfort is one thing, complacency is another. We can strive for a comfort level with acceptance of procedures, approaches and steps for moving forward. If we keep away from being complacent with just the "we have always done it that way" mentality, we can feel good about a place, situation or approach. Because of the outcome, the plan of effectiveness will lead to a personal, earned comfort.

Similarly, when things, people, ideas, change, etc. do not initially feel good or do not resonate with us,

154

it is a far greater challenge to be open to accepting, incorporating or adopting and adapting to those things.

Being somewhat patient with the bailout process over the next 60 days, and very impatient with what has happened in the past, will allow you to look at what works and how to learn about what does not "sit well with it". This will enable the chance for the construction zone to be your place for your bailout.

Make it Happen!

If you have ever volunteered for a political campaign, you've likely discovered the chaotic scene that exists in the waning days leading up to Election Day. In one corner of the campaign headquarters you'll see a table full of volunteers making phone calls. Another table full of helpers may be working on some type of mailing. Meanwhile, the phones are ringing off the hook while supporters stream in and out picking up yard signs or other collateral materials. You may wonder how all of this activity gets off the ground.

We in the industry sometimes describe campaigns as organized chaos. In the final days before an election, there are so many different moving parts and different programs being conducted simultaneously, it seems the only strategy for a campaign manager or candidate is to simply hold on tight and roll with the flow.

Contrast this scene to that of the first few days of a campaign. When there are only one or two people sitting around a table thinking, "Ok, we need to wage a campaign; now what?"

The chaos of the final days didn't occur organically. Before there was organized chaos there was orchestrated chaos. Nothing happened that the campaign manager and others didn't make happen.

The same principal holds true for most any endeavor. Although we may look at large or successful organizations or efforts and be overwhelmed by what they have accomplished and wonder how we can duplicate such success, all great organizations and efforts began with someone saying, "Ok, now what?" Somebody made something happen.

Rome wasn't built in a day, but one day someone laid the first brick. Rome didn't suddenly build itself.

Nothing happens unless you make it happen. So, go ahead, make your bailout plan finally come together in form and format…make it happen!

Bailout and Beyond Tip #8
Stop Trying...Start Doing!

Isn't it interesting how acceptable someone saying "I'm trying to XYZ" is? What I mean is, we often nod and smile after hearing "I'm trying to balance my work/life better", or "I'm trying to be more patient", or even "I'm trying to get better at names", when in fact, what we are really thinking (if we are engaged fully in that conversation) is that is lame..."you are trying"...I will see how that works for you. Right? No? If not, then you are likely simply a "Try-er", too!

Try-ers are people who do not fully commit to things, engage totally or even make a true effort. Try-ers want an excuse for what might not go well. Try-ers are fearful...of disappointing you, themselves or someone along the way.

Think about it...how many times does someone who tells you they are going to "try" to join a function, group or party actually join? It is so infrequent; you will likely have few recollections of it occurring.

As a matter of fact, I prefer invitations/requests only offer a yes or no reply. Some of the wonderful and convenient online resources for invitations and announcements provide the cowardly "maybe", which is just a more direct form of "I'll try", or "I am waiting to see if I get a better offer". I consider every maybe or "I'll try" to be a no, and write off that person as a committed or potentially committed attendee. If, in fact someone replies "maybe" or "I'll try" often enough, they are best served to be removed from my invitation list…and yours, too. By continuing to include them, you are forcing their weak position to another point of non-committal, non-truth where they are not strong enough to say "no, thank you", and rather give the lame, often insulting "I'll try" or "maybe".

If you are the "Try-er" in your group, you have created a false sense of honesty and openness with your friends/colleagues because your word is devalued. Each time you give a weak response or offer a weak statement voluntarily in conversation, you are feeding the other people's conscious or subconscious notions that you are, in fact, not in control of your decisions, focus or time.

Wow! All that from a simple "I'll try"? Yes. Be smart, straight-forward and honest with people when asked for a response or reply. I have heard people rationalize "try-er" behavior as they do not want to be rude, or they do not want to hurt other people's feelings…really? How is it kind, thoughtful or real to suggest you will make an effort, when in fact, you will not? Your character and self-respect should be worth more to you. And, if that is not the case, the people with whom you are surrounding yourself may warrant a higher degree of professional and personal thoughtfulness based on their character.

You've probably "tried" to make changes before this book was written, maybe yourself, maybe with others, or even with other books, so, what do you replace your wishy-washy verbiage with when you are tempted to "try"? I say stop trying, and start doing. A few scenarios are outlined here:

When you would like to do something, yet do not have all the details, say "I am saying no at this point, as I'm not in a position to say yes. As soon as I have the details on XYZ (the babysitter, the guests I have coming in, my work schedule, etc.), I will get back to you. And, then, actually get back to that person (minimally five days prior to the event...see page 66, Availability, for further details).

If though, you are just not interested, resist providing excuses, and state "No, thank you." or "No, and thank you for asking," and let it be. If the person/people want to know the reason, they are crossing the line. At that point, you owe them nothing.

In the case where you are doing something new, such as learning a language, engaging in a new endeavor, etc., creating your bailout, it is suggested that you convey that by saying "I am in the process of bailing myself out", which is strong and clear, as opposed to verbalizing "I am trying to get out of this situation", as that is nearly hopeless and less than positive. Another way to express something similar is by saying "I am taking action through the book *Hey, Where's My Bailout?* to create a new approach to life." The ideal way to say it shows direction and offers solid information to those who are listening.

Imagine if you are *trying* to finish this book. Think again, and be in the process of reading and implementing the entire book (and you are almost done, by the way!)!

Ellis Traub – The Investor's Toolkit™

It's never too late in life to create your own bailout plan. Just ask 78 year-old Ellis Traub, designer and developer of The Investor's Toolkit™ and founder and Chairman of the Board of Inve$tWare Corporation™.

In 1972, with four sons nearing college age, Ellis realized that his savings were inadequate to finance their education. He had saved too little, and had poorly managed what little he had saved. Ellis decided he needed to "catch up."

On the advice of a stockbroker "friend," Ellis invested his entire savings in one rapidly rising stock. He also borrowed on his holdings to buy more (bought on margin) and bought still more on borrowed credit.

161

He bet it all on the market, and the market tanked. All that remained was Ellis' house, his job and a very considerable debt.

So Ellis picked himself up and continued on with his job of piloting planes for Eastern Airlines. When Ellis retired in 1987 as a Lockheed 1101 Captain, and having flown 31 years for Eastern Airlines, he decided to accept his pension in one lump sum.

"Fortunately, I didn't have access to my pension fund in 1972 or I might have lost all of that too," jokes Ellis. Fifteen years after losing everything, he decided to give investing one more shot.

Ellis happened upon a newspaper article one day that mentioned an upcoming seminar on how to evaluate common stocks. The seminar was being offered by the National Association of Investors Corporation (NAIC) – a non-profit organization whose goal was to empower individual investors and investment club members to invest successfully in commons stocks.

Ellis attended the NAIC seminar that Saturday, and his life changed forever.

"I was fascinated by the organization's elegant, yet simple, methodology," says Ellis. "When I returned home that afternoon, I sat at my computer and entered all of the formulas and calculations that I had just learned into a spreadsheet. By that night I was able to duplicate the tasks required to analyze a stock for prospective purchase. From then on I was hooked."

As he attended more workshops and mastered the NAIC methodology, Ellis continued to refine his spreadsheet until it grew into a full-fledged stock analysis program which he named Take$tock. With Ellis' permission, NAIC soon began to market his Take$tock software to its members.

The program was so well received that NAIC then retained Ellis to develop its own official software product and The Investor's Toolkit™ was born. Today, many thousands of investors use The Investor's Toolkit™ to help them analyze prospective stock transactions, and each day another 20 to 30 new members are added to the list.

"Whereas once I was concerned about how long I might live before my funds ran out, now I could live forever – at least in terms of financial security," says Ellis. "And I chalk it all up to what I learned from NAIC."

We also chalk it up to Ellis' decision to act.

Ellis' latest project is a blog. His intention is to convince the public that intelligent investing need not be a losing proposition and is within everyone's ability to do without professional help.

"Unfortunately," says Traub, "the securities industry, which profits from every purchase and sale, has succeeded in convincing people that 'investing' means betting on the stock market. So they must buy and sell frequently to try to outguess that market. This, of course, does far more to enrich the securities industry than the hapless 'investor.'"

His point will be, of course, that those who recognize that owning pieces of well-managed companies can ignore the market and profit from their ownership, regardless of what "the herd" chooses to do. And he will provide his readers with all the tools they will need to do it for themselves.

You will find Ellis' blog at www.financialiteracy.us.

Putting It All Together

Here you are at the fifth, and final, step of *Hey, Where's My Bailout?* Do you have a bailout? Do you have a plan? Maybe it seems like yes, maybe it seems like no. You have read a lot about preparation and opportunity, completed (many) activities, and learned of individual accounts of success, but the moment of truth, *or step, in this case*, is now upon you.

You DO have a bailout plan in place, although you may not see it as such as it is spotty and fragmented in its format and flow. The time has come to put it all together into one comprehensive plan that you can follow, track and review to ensure you stay the course. This is the reason for the last part of the book…your Bailout Plan 60 Day Calendar.

Your Bailout Plan 60 Day Calendar will position you to act, act, act each day. You have already made a great deal of progress, but now you will take all the lessons, growth, insights and ideas from *Assess, Prioritize, Leverage* and *Communicate* and pull them together to finish your bailout plan.

Reflect back to the previous chapters, where you considered your Life Areas, Cycle of Self, Availability and Strengths & Opportunities. You also determined your Planned Accomplishments, Areas of Expertise, NETWORKing Opportunities, Circle of Trust, and 30-Second Pitch.

All of these activities have led you here…to the point where your plan culminates in an action-oriented guide for you – for *your* bailout. You have done all of the necessary preparation - now here is your final opportunity to bring together your bailout plan!

Pause to reflect for just a moment on all you have already done. Think back to the inspirational personal stories you read. As with the people in the stories, you, and you alone, are responsible for creating your own preparation and opportunity. Remember Casey Wohl? She did not overlook her assessment. Jenn Ingallinera strove to prioritize and went elsewhere for greater happiness. Sean Winton leveraged opportunities and created his own unique offering, and Domingo Quintero communicated clearly and consistently to create his success. Similarly, Ellis Traub brought it all together and acted to create his own bailout plan.

Already you are in the *Act* mode…you have been ever since you purchased this book. It is important to ensure you are being productive and not just busy. You can busy yourself with activities that amount to little or no results, or you can be productive in a short amount of time while creating significant, lasting results. Given the choice the latter of the two is the obvious…and where you are now. You are ready to start creating action, not just motion in your life.

Step 5: Act encompasses everything you have already done, and takes it to a higher level - one of commitment, movement and results. After all, a great idea without action is just a thought, but a great idea with action drives results!

Your Bailout Plan 60 Day Calendar takes lessons from the first four steps and incorporates them into your bailout plan. All of the previous activities and worksheets can stand on their own, but the summation of these activities is greater than the individual parts and is a final roadmap for success – a formula that you can apply to different challenges and situations to create a bailout plan to meet your specific needs, whatever they may be.

With just this one last step left, here you go…

How the Bailout Plan 60 Day Calendar Works

The Bailout Plan 60 Day Calendar is structured and flows from day to day. There are two copies of the Calendar: use the first Calendar to layout your entire bailout plan in 60 days, and then use the second Calendar to adjust and update your plan each week.

Because you will be creating your bailout plan at a specific time in your life, use a pen (so that your commitment is less likely to be pushed or erased) and write specific dates in the ⬚ / ⬚ part of the calendar. Now that you have your start and finish date on paper, you have already taken action and are ready for more.

Just as you list your starting and ending dates, you will want to establish your starting and ending goals and actions. As we discussed in *Step 1: Assess*, a roadmap is only effective if we know the beginning and ending points of our trip. Your Life Area Planned Accomplishments are the ending points to your bailout plan. Go now to the 60th day of your Calendar and write your Life Area Planned Accomplishment for that day. Beginning with the end in mind, you can now begin to complete your bailout plan.

Let's go back to your Life Area Planned Accomplishment on page 106, where you selected the three areas you want to target (if you have less than three that is ok - the instructions will only change slightly in that your actions will equal your number of Life Areas Planned Accomplishments).

168

Your Life Areas are the catalyst for each daily action. For your three Life Areas selected, you noted three actions to complete. For each of those actions, you are one day closer to realizing your Planned Accomplishments!

Having each Life Area Planned Accomplishments' activity done from *Step 3: Leverage*, you will now just insert your First Steps from page 106 into your calendar. Those three First Steps will be the first Actions of your Bailout Plan 60 Day Calendar. You will create the rest of your Actions as stepping stones that get you from your First Steps to your Life Area Planned Accomplishments. Create three Actions for yourself each day…for all 60 days. (If you feel a bit overwhelmed or confused, please don't worry. This first calendar you create is just a draft. Remember, you will be able to revise and edit your calendar each week.)

Next, write a clear Focus for each and every day. A clear Focus states action such as "make a contact at company xyz," not "call company xyz," or "eat 1,200 calories of lean protein and complex carbohydrates," instead of "eat better."

Be specific and eliminate qualifiers - those ambiguous words like "more," "better," "faster," or "slower." This will keep you out of the trap of only making small changes or improvements, or none at all, due to feeling busy versus being truly productive (motion versus action.)

Imagine if you said you wanted to "call company xyz," and you did, but did not get through - you would have succeeded in your Focus. Contrarily, a

Focus of "making contact at company xyz" means you will stick with it until you get a response. *This is staying focused.* In the small space provided, you may abbreviate or shorten your Focus, but make sure it is clear to you and carries accountability. After all, this is *your* bailout plan!

In the draft form of your Bailout Plan 60 Day Calendar, you will not have anything listed for Went Well. As a draft that you complete ahead of time, things have not yet happened. Once you begin to live your Calendar, you will likely find that some Actions worked better than others. Use the Weekly Review sheets to help *Assess*, *Prioritize*, *Leverage* and *Communicate* changes and adjustments to your Bailout Plan 60 Day Calendar.

Your Bailout Plan 60 Day Calendar
First 30 Days Draft

Bailout Calendar

Life Areas: 1) Career/Work 2) Communication 3) Direction

Sunday	Monday	Tuesday	Wednesday	Thursday	Friday	Saturday
Date ►Focus / Action 1) / Action 2) / Action 3) / √ Went Well	Date ►Focus / Action 1) / Action 2) / Action 3) / √ Went Well	Date ►Focus / Action 1) / Action 2) / Action 3) / √ Went Well	Date ►Focus / Action 1) / Action 2) / Action 3) / √ Went Well	Date ►Focus / Action 1) / Action 2) / Action 3) / √ Went Well	Date ►Focus / Action 1) / Action 2) / Action 3) / √ Went Well	Date ►Focus / Action 1) / Action 2) / Action 3) / √ Went Well
1 ► 1) 2) 3) √	8/31 ►Document 1) online search 2) strengths 3) list enjoyable √	9/1 ►Internal ideas 1) 1 hour research 2) opportunities 3) categorize list √	9/2 Breakdown ►Barriers 1) List fears 2) List to ask 3) 10 min. meditate √	9/3 ►External feedback meetup 1) Sue 2) Ask Sue 3) Gratitude journal √	9/4 Company ►Contact 1) call former mgr. 2) Ask for feedback 3) Consider Options √	9/5 personal goal 1) work accomplish. 2) Register for class 3) review life areas √
9/6 ►forward progress 1) internal post. 2) Write a letter 3) note something I enjoy √	9/7 ►Idea sharing 1) ask mgr. 2) class 3) 10 min med √	9/8 one ►accomplish. 1) document work 2) review letter 3) list of happy people √	9/9 Talk w/ ►family 1) Budget 2) lead mtg 3) 10 min. med. √	9/10 ►ask at work 1) 360° feedback 2) Well/Impr. 3) Career Path √	9/11 ►Be proactive 1) meet HR 2) send letter 3) 10 min. med. √	9/12 ►Stop avoiding 1) Print Resume 2) record self 3) list of contacts √
9/13 ►Hit goal 1) New Resume 1 hour 2) share idea A-J in mtg. 3) Pursue new hobby √	9/14 ►celebrate Success 1) Resume done 2) class 3) research ideas √	9/15 ►Look forward 1) Resume fit. 2) review recording 3) check on courses √	9/16 Talk to ►3 1) send resume 2) lead mtg 3) 10 min med. √	9/17 ask right ►questions 1) Followup feedback 2) class 3) review finances √	9/18 ►Get moving 1) schedule info. int. 2) recording assess 3) bills √	9/19 ►Reflection Int. ?s 1) 2) review feedback 3) budget √
9/20 ►Social skills 1) talk w/ brother offer to 2) assist in mtg 3) read blogs √	9/21 contact ►3 connect 1) @ networking 2) class 3) set up blog √	9/22 ►speak my mind 1) meet w/ mgr. contact 2) class member 3) blog √	9/23 Ask ►forgiveness Amends 1) w/ mktg 2) lead mtg review 3) budget √	9/24 Look ►forward schedule 1) mtg 2) class assess 3) progress √	9/25 ►set plan networking 1) contact 2) class mentor decide 3) on class √	9/26 ►look for partners 1) Fit on network. 2) review feedback ask if 3) friends will join √
9/27 ►read 1) 1 hour online 2) blaterinam 3) Blog √	9/28 ►research 1) 1 hr online 2) class 3) 10 min med √	9/29 ►reflect 1) match for roles. 2) meet HR Review 3) list √	1 ► 1) 2) 3) √	1 ► 1) 2) 3) √	1 ► 1) 2) 3) √	1 ► 1) 2) 3) √

171

You may consider some of your Draft Calendar postings to be incomplete, weak, too narrow or too broad, but it is important that you *Act* to put something down in writing. The draft is not about right or wrong, it is about establishing plans, procedures and systems that get you to your Life Area Planned Accomplishments.

You will create a draft for Month One and Month Two. You can start at any time of the month and on any day, but we recommend your weeks run Monday – Sunday.

You should complete your Weekly Reviews each Sunday. Remember - a good Monday begins on Sunday. Start your week strong. We crafted the Bailout Calendar in the traditional Sunday start format to remind you to do your proper planning for each week.

Now it's your turn. Complete the following Bailout Plan 60 Day Calendar drafts, and then move onto the Weekly Reviews:

Your Bailout Plan 60 Day Calendar
First 30 Days Draft

Bailout Calendar

Life Areas: 1)_____ 2)_____ 3)_____

Sunday	Monday	Tuesday	Wednesday	Thursday	Friday	Saturday
Date	Date	Date	Date	Date	Date	Date
►Focus	►Focus	►Focus	►Focus	►Focus	►Focus	►Focus
Action 1)	Action 1)	Action 1)	Action 1)	Action 1)	Action 1)	Action 1)
Action 2)	Action 2)	Action 2)	Action 2)	Action 2)	Action 2)	Action 2)
Action 3)	Action 3)	Action 3)	Action 3)	Action 3)	Action 3)	Action 3)
√ Went Well	√ Went Well	√ Went Well	√ Went Well	√ Went Well	√ Went Well	√ Went Well
/	/	/	/	/	/	/
►	►	►	►	►	►	►
1)	1)	1)	1)	1)	1)	1)
2)	2)	2)	2)	2)	2)	2)
3)	3)	3)	3)	3)	3)	3)
√	√	√	√	√	√	√
/	/	/	/	/	/	/
►	►	►	►	►	►	►
1)	1)	1)	1)	1)	1)	1)
2)	2)	2)	2)	2)	2)	2)
3)	3)	3)	3)	3)	3)	3)
√	√	√	√	√	√	√
/	/	/	/	/	/	/
►	►	►	►	►	►	►
1)	1)	1)	1)	1)	1)	1)
2)	2)	2)	2)	2)	2)	2)
3)	3)	3)	3)	3)	3)	3)
√	√	√	√	√	√	√
/	/	/	/	/	/	/
►	►	►	►	►	►	►
1)	1)	1)	1)	1)	1)	1)
2)	2)	2)	2)	2)	2)	2)
3)	3)	3)	3)	3)	3)	3)
√	√	√	√	√	√	√
/	/	/	/	/	/	/
►	►	►	►	►	►	►
1)	1)	1)	1)	1)	1)	1)
2)	2)	2)	2)	2)	2)	2)
3)	3)	3)	3)	3)	3)	3)
√	√	√	√	√	√	√

173

Your Bailout Plan 60 Day Calendar
Second 30 Days Draft

Bailout Calendar

Life Areas: 1)_____ 2)_____ 3)_____

Sunday	Monday	Tuesday	Wednesday	Thursday	Friday	Saturday
Date	Date	Date	Date	Date	Date	Date
►Focus	►Focus	►Focus	►Focus	►Focus	►Focus	►Focus
Action 1)	Action 1)	Action 1)	Action 1)	Action 1)	Action 1)	Action 1)
Action 2)	Action 2)	Action 2)	Action 2)	Action 2)	Action 2)	Action 2)
Action 3)	Action 3)	Action 3)	Action 3)	Action 3)	Action 3)	Action 3)
√ Went Well	√ Went Well	√ Went Well	√ Went Well	√ Went Well	√ Went Well	√ Went Well
/	/	/	/	/	/	/
►	►	►	►	►	►	►
1)	1)	1)	1)	1)	1)	1)
2)	2)	2)	2)	2)	2)	2)
3)	3)	3)	3)	3)	3)	3)
√	√	√	√	√	√	√
/	/	/	/	/	/	/
►	►	►	►	►	►	►
1)	1)	1)	1)	1)	1)	1)
2)	2)	2)	2)	2)	2)	2)
3)	3)	3)	3)	3)	3)	3)
√	√	√	√	√	√	√
/	/	/	/	/	/	/
►	►	►	►	►	►	►
1)	1)	1)	1)	1)	1)	1)
2)	2)	2)	2)	2)	2)	2)
3)	3)	3)	3)	3)	3)	3)
√	√	√	√	√	√	√
/	/	/	/	/	/	/
►	►	►	►	►	►	►
1)	1)	1)	1)	1)	1)	1)
2)	2)	2)	2)	2)	2)	2)
3)	3)	3)	3)	3)	3)	3)
√	√	√	√	√	√	√
/	/	/	/	/	/	/
►	►	►	►	►	►	►
1)	1)	1)	1)	1)	1)	1)
2)	2)	2)	2)	2)	2)	2)
3)	3)	3)	3)	3)	3)	3)
√	√	√	√	√	√	√

174

Weekly Reviews allow you to delve even deeper into your bailout plan - they are designed so that you have plenty of space for writing. Use the Weekly Reviews to note changes (we have noted changes with a star) to your draft Calendar. Once you have completed a Weekly Review, update your final Calendar for that week.

Here is an example:

Weekly Review for Bailout Calendar

Life Areas: 1) Career/Work 2) Communication 3) Direction

Day	Focus	Action 1)	Action 2)	Action 3)
✷ Monday 9/7	Make noticable progress in each focus area by sharing internally + externally	review internal postings and minimally post for one.	write a letter to someone in circle of trust level one or two	note something I enjoy + reflect on how that ties to my direction
✷ Tuesday 9/8	Sharing ideas internally + externally for clarity	ask manager for things I do well + thing to improve in meetings	attend class + listen to gain new information	use 10 minutes of meditation to reflect on enjoyment + appreciation
✷ Wednesday 9/9	noting accomplishments and recognizing self.	Document a success at work + update resume to reflect it.	review letter for clarity, intent + clear communication (meeting cancelled)	(already made list of people) schedule coffee or lunch w/ happy, well directed person
✷ Thursday 9/10	ask for feedback at work + with family	share budget at home w/family members for ideas	(meeting cancelled was rescheduled) lead meeting + survey attendees	meditate regarding career/path + plans.
✷ Friday 9/11	Be proactive in getting ideas across + assessing opportunities	meet w/ HR to discuss options + school + banks	send updated letter seeking ideas on trust + communication	Commit to something suggested in HR meeting + meditation
Saturday 9/12	Stop avoiding issues	print resume examples	use camera to record myself giving presentation	Make an action plan for each list of contacts
Sunday 9/13	Hit 2 week goal	work 1 hour on new resume	plan to share positive idea in meeting. Prepare for it.	Think of hobby ideas + how to pursue them.

175

Finally, compare what you initially planned with what you are now committed to Act upon for the week. The final Calendar is where you will note what Went Well for each day. Nine (9) Weekly Reviews are included in your book. Complete one Review each Sunday in order to best prepare your week, and to give yourself the best opportunity to make progress in your bailout plan.

Weekly Review Week 1

Weekly Review for Bailout Calendar				
Life Areas: 1)_____ 2)_____ 3)_____				
Day	**Focus**	**Action 1)**	**Action 2)**	**Action 3)**
Monday /				
Tuesday /				
Wednesday /				
Thursday /				
Friday /				
Saturday /				
Sunday /				

Your Bailout Plan 60 Day Calendar
First 30 Days

Bailout Calendar

Life Areas: 1)_____ 2)_____ 3)_____

Sunday	Monday	Tuesday	Wednesday	Thursday	Friday	Saturday
Date	Date	Date	Date	Date	Date	Date
▶Focus	▶Focus	▶Focus	▶Focus	▶Focus	▶Focus	▶Focus
Action 1)	Action 1)	Action 1)	Action 1)	Action 1)	Action 1)	Action 1)
Action 2)	Action 2)	Action 2)	Action 2)	Action 2)	Action 2)	Action 2)
Action 3)	Action 3)	Action 3)	Action 3)	Action 3)	Action 3)	Action 3)
√ Went Well	√ Went Well	√ Went Well	√ Went Well	√ Went Well	√ Went Well	√ Went Well
/	/	/	/	/	/	/
▶	▶	▶	▶	▶	▶	▶
1)	1)	1)	1)	1)	1)	1)
2)	2)	2)	2)	2)	2)	2)
3)	3)	3)	3)	3)	3)	3)
√	√	√	√	√	√	√
/	/	/	/	/	/	/
▶	▶	▶	▶	▶	▶	▶
1)	1)	1)	1)	1)	1)	1)
2)	2)	2)	2)	2)	2)	2)
3)	3)	3)	3)	3)	3)	3)
√	√	√	√	√	√	√
/	/	/	/	/	/	/
▶	▶	▶	▶	▶	▶	▶
1)	1)	1)	1)	1)	1)	1)
2)	2)	2)	2)	2)	2)	2)
3)	3)	3)	3)	3)	3)	3)
√	√	√	√	√	√	√
/	/	/	/	/	/	/
▶	▶	▶	▶	▶	▶	▶
1)	1)	1)	1)	1)	1)	1)
2)	2)	2)	2)	2)	2)	2)
3)	3)	3)	3)	3)	3)	3)
√	√	√	√	√	√	√
/	/	/	/	/	/	/
▶	▶	▶	▶	▶	▶	▶
1)	1)	1)	1)	1)	1)	1)
2)	2)	2)	2)	2)	2)	2)
3)	3)	3)	3)	3)	3)	3)
√	√	√	√	√	√	√

Your Bailout Plan 60 Day Calendar
Second 30 Days

Bailout Calendar

Life Areas: 1)_____ 2)_____ 3)_____

Sunday	Monday	Tuesday	Wednesday	Thursday	Friday	Saturday
Date	Date	Date	Date	Date	Date	Date
►Focus	►Focus	►Focus	►Focus	►Focus	►Focus	►Focus
Action 1)	Action 1)	Action 1)	Action 1)	Action 1)	Action 1)	Action 1)
Action 2)	Action 2)	Action 2)	Action 2)	Action 2)	Action 2)	Action 2)
Action 3)	Action 3)	Action 3)	Action 3)	Action 3)	Action 3)	Action 3)
√ Went Well	√ Went Well	√ Went Well	√ Went Well	√ Went Well	√ Went Well	√ Went Well
/	/	/	/	/	/	/
►	►	►	►	►	►	►
1)	1)	1)	1)	1)	1)	1)
2)	2)	2)	2)	2)	2)	2)
3)	3)	3)	3)	3)	3)	3)
√	√	√	√	√	√	√
/	/	/	/	/	/	/
►	►	►	►	►	►	►
1)	1)	1)	1)	1)	1)	1)
2)	2)	2)	2)	2)	2)	2)
3)	3)	3)	3)	3)	3)	3)
√	√	√	√	√	√	√
/	/	/	/	/	/	/
►	►	►	►	►	►	►
1)	1)	1)	1)	1)	1)	1)
2)	2)	2)	2)	2)	2)	2)
3)	3)	3)	3)	3)	3)	3)
√	√	√	√	√	√	√
/	/	/	/	/	/	/
►	►	►	►	►	►	►
1)	1)	1)	1)	1)	1)	1)
2)	2)	2)	2)	2)	2)	2)
3)	3)	3)	3)	3)	3)	3)
√	√	√	√	√	√	√
/	/	/	/	/	/	/
►	►	►	►	►	►	►
1)	1)	1)	1)	1)	1)	1)
2)	2)	2)	2)	2)	2)	2)
3)	3)	3)	3)	3)	3)	3)
√	√	√	√	√	√	√

Weekly Review Week 2

Weekly Review for Bailout Calendar				
Life Areas: 1)_____ 2)_____ 3)_____				
Day	Focus	Action 1)	Action 2)	Action 3)
Monday /				
Tuesday /				
Wednesday /				
Thursday /				
Friday /				
Saturday /				
Sunday /				

Weekly Review Week 3

	Weekly Review for Bailout Calendar			
Life Areas: 1)_____	2)_____		3)_____	
Day	Focus	Action 1)	Action 2)	Action 3)
Monday /				
Tuesday /				
Wednesday /				
Thursday /				
Friday /				
Saturday /				
Sunday /				

Weekly Review Week 4

Day	Focus	Action 1)	Action 2)	Action 3)
Weekly Review for Bailout Calendar				
Life Areas: 1)_____ 2)_____ 3)_____				
Monday /				
Tuesday /				
Wednesday /				
Thursday /				
Friday /				
Saturday /				
Sunday /				

Weekly Review Week 5

Weekly Review for Bailout Calendar				
Life Areas: 1)_____ 2)_____ 3)_____				
Day	Focus	Action 1)	Action 2)	Action 3)
Monday /				
Tuesday /				
Wednesday /				
Thursday /				
Friday /				
Saturday /				
Sunday /				

Weekly Review Week 6

	Weekly Review for Bailout Calendar			
	Life Areas: 1)_____ 2)_____ 3)_____			
Day	**Focus**	**Action 1)**	**Action 2)**	**Action 3)**
Monday /				
Tuesday /				
Wednesday /				
Thursday /				
Friday /				
Saturday /				
Sunday /				

Weekly Review Week 7

Weekly Review for Bailout Calendar

Life Areas: 1)_____ 2)_____ 3)_____

Day	Focus	Action 1)	Action 2)	Action 3)
Monday /				
Tuesday /				
Wednesday /				
Thursday /				
Friday /				
Saturday /				
Sunday /				

Weekly Review Week 8

	Weekly Review for Bailout Calendar			
	Life Areas: 1)_____ 2)_____ 3)_____			
Day	**Focus**	**Action 1)**	**Action 2)**	**Action 3)**
Monday /				
Tuesday /				
Wednesday /				
Thursday /				
Friday /				
Saturday /				
Sunday /				

Weekly Review Week 9

Weekly Review for Bailout Calendar				
Life Areas: 1)_____ 2)_____ 3)_____				
Day	Focus	Action 1)	Action 2)	Action 3)
Monday /				
Tuesday /				
Wednesday /				
Thursday /				
Friday /				
Saturday /				
Sunday /				

Epilogue

At the time of writing, the collective cry across our nation of *"Hey, Where's My Bailout?"* has grown increasingly louder. Some of the world's largest financial institutions, having already received billions in taxpayer-funded emergency loans, are returning back for even more. Bailout figures that seemed absurdly high only months ago seem pedestrian now when compared to many of the staggering requests. How many bailouts will we see and how high will the figures rise? Just like the spendthrift lottery winner or the reckless athlete, it seems that the money never lasts - no matter how large the bailout amounts that are given to these failing institutions.

These are anxious and uncertain times for sure. Consumer confidence is at an all time low, as people look towards their future with many questions and even more doubts. Now, more than at any point in most of our lifetimes, people are seeking safe havens in the midst of a storm – a roadmap that can guide their lives towards prosperity and happiness.

But you know the secret to finding such a roadmap. You have the plans, procedures and systems needed to create your own bailout and carve out your own destiny. Regardless of the circumstance, your map is timeless, and you can bail yourself out of any situation, in any area of your life, in any economy.

You understand that good fortune outcome is subject largely to probability, and that you can maximize the probability of achieving good fortune through preparation and creation of opportunity through:

- **Assessing** how prior preparations, or lack thereof, led you to your current point in life,

- **Prioritizing** what types of preparation you need to best pursue the opportunities you seek,

- **Leveraging** your preparation to create or expand new opportunities,

- **Communicating** and creating more opportunity by allowing others to assist you, and by

- **Acting**, because you alone are responsible for creating your preparation and opportunity, and therefore, your bailout.

You have discovered the formula to your own success. You possess the tools necessary to create your own bailout for your own unique situation. And you can do it in just 60 days.

Vision and planning are interconnected - one will always fail without the other. You likely have always possessed the vision for success, and now through your reading and application, you have the planning as well...*your own personal bailout plan.*

Congratulations, the rest is up to you to make it happen!

"You must take personal responsibility. You cannot change the circumstances, the seasons, or the wind, but you can change yourself. That is something you have charge of."

~ Jim Rohn

Footnote: Thank you for investing in you! For additional tips and tools, or for booking speaking engagements, appearances, and interviews regarding this book or other topics, as well as inquiring on special rates on large quantities of this book or other books, please contact the authors through http://www.HeyWheresMyBailout.com .

www.ingramcontent.com/pod-product-compliance
Lightning Source LLC
Chambersburg PA
CBHW031256090426
42742CB00007B/479